THE HUMAN CONDITION

Valentin Matcas, M.Ed.

DEDICATION

I dedicate this book to everyone eager to learn and develop
continuously throughout life.

CONTENTS

1 Human Conditions Influencing Your Life   1

2 Natural Conditions of the Natural Environment   24

3 Systematic Social Human Conditions   90

4 You as a Human Condition in Life and in the World   129

1 HUMAN CONDITIONS INFLUENCING YOUR LIFE

The human condition is the print or manner in which you and humanity influence those around, the human environment, the entire world, and Life herself. Furthermore, the specific human conditions that you enhance yourself come back to influence you similarly, knowingly or unknowingly. You always interconnect with this world as best as you can, favorably or unfavorably, as those around allow you, only to be able to fulfill your needs. As you study history closely, you notice how some people chose to die than to become dreadful conditions in this world, while others never cared, and now this is their world. Consequently, there are always tyrants throughout the upper layers of society seeking to be the worst conditions possible in this world, only to debilitate this world, rendering it controllable, discriminatory, and therefore exploitable, just for them to have someone to make their beds, polish their shoes, pour their drinks, and button their shirts. They destroy an entire world, while making the human condition dreadful in this world, for them to have servants and slaves, since this is the current human condition in an undeveloped consensual world.

Just as you remain aware of all environmental conditions influencing your own fulfillment and condition in life, in society, and in this world, you should remain aware of all conditions that you leave behind through your own life and behavior. Just as life copes with the environment throughout a continuous toil as science describes, the environment is alive itself, it is part of life, it is made of life, and it includes you, along with your loved ones, and your entire condition and contribution to this world. Yet if you give in and you see your environment as a continuously challenging harmful condition since this is what science states, then you engage in win-lose interactions with the environment unnecessarily, while the environment is similar to you, formed of life, humans, and the entire human world.

If you become an unfavorable condition of this world by engaging in win-lose interactions with this world knowingly or unknowingly, the entire world has to cope with you as an unfavorable condition, exactly as science states. While as an unfavorable condition in this world, you do not stand a chance, because you are one and they are an entire world, always against you. Unless you are organized in this world, the favorable against the unfavorable, or the people against the people, which in itself is the worst unfavorable human condition in this world: humans against humans, and souls against souls.

Life, this world, and the human society are very complex, swinging continuously with and against you, since your environment is filled with conditions that are good, bad, favorable, unfavorable, natural, and consensual, as it is important to identify, predict, and control them.

Throughout this book, we study the human condition along with all environmental conditions influencing the human existence, as the human condition in life and in this world, the human social condition, and the human higher conditions. We also identify all favorable and unfavorable existential elements along with their consequences, for a better fulfillment.

What human conditions exactly are we considering, and

why are these so important in life and in the world? Conditions are everywhere, human, natural, social, living, consensual, and higher, found throughout all your environments, inner, outside, and higher. Because you never live your life out in the nonexistent, but you live your life within worlds and realities consisting your environment in all its details. These environmental details form your environment altogether, and may by determined, defined, triggered, or created through natural, consensual, or supreme laws or living circumstances. Some of these environmental details are conditions or even niche elements, but only those affecting you, positively or negatively.

Together, your favorable conditions form your human niche. This is how the human conditions are favorable and unfavorable, since they come from the environment, or you may trigger them or place them in the environment yourself. Others do the same, individually or organized in entire groups and societies, and together, these form the human condition.

You can even feel the human condition, since its presence remains with you in the background of your cognition. Only drugs can mask it sometimes, but very shortly, and with dreadful consequences. While you may see the human condition directly, since it has its specific look as it marks your face permanently, making it happy, sad, angry or at peace. Everybody can see it well, since that is your own human condition in life, in this world, in society, and even in your inner world.

This is the general human condition, formed of all available human conditions. Many times, people are happy or angry with their authorities, because these decide their human condition continuously on their behalf, while these authorities have their own authorities above, part of an entire consensual social hierarchy. Yet society does not hold all the human conditions, even though the current human society could certainly make a difference in life and in this world, if it is only allowed. Since in general, the climate where you live is an important condition, along with the availability of food, adequate transportation, sources of income, social relationships, laws, crimes, sources of entertainment, safety, sources of knowledge, opportunities, and means of development.

These are only the obvious conditions influencing the human condition, while you are one of these conditions yourself. Additionally, there are the hidden or less considered human conditions, as the multitude of consensual beliefs and stereotypes found everywhere, along with various consensual agreements favoring or disadvantaging you knowingly or not, meant to discriminate you or even to exploit you, since exploitation is a major current human condition. It is worse when you are made to harm and exploit this world similarly, since you become a negative condition in this world yourself. When it happens, this world takes you down eventually, regardless of what you are promised, only to leave tyrants behind, who do similarly.

Because this world is not formed only of the Masses as science depicts, but it contains the Brotherhood just as well. These are significantly more numerous and more demanding that the Masses, and they decide all conditions in this world, while placing themselves in win-lose interconnections with the rest of this world, many times deliberately, since this is the direct or implicit requirement in the current consensual Brotherhood. This organized unfavorable consensual condition takes humanity to its common grave, in an extraordinary funeral march, with most of this world marching in ignorant joy, since this is the ideology, and now this is the human condition.

There are many brotherhoods consisting the current consensual Brotherhood, some criminal and some legal, some financial and some religious, and some even spiritual, while all seeking social control and material profit, or this is the general belief, because people will always join brotherhoods of any kind only to be able to fulfill their needs easier and with more certainty, or depending on their developmental level, people may join brotherhoods for knowledge and continuous development at the third, intelligent human level, or to help them feel even better at their zero, addictive level, or to help them ascend socially at their second, animal level.

Yet regardless of circumstances, as long as their fulfillment is not natural, as long as they do not fulfill Life and the human society, they remain consensual, at the first servitude tyrannical level, and this harms the world. It is important to be able to identify your human condition if you are part of a group, brotherhood, or entire society, because you have additional, comprehensive conditions in this manner, different than what you encounter and leave behind as you live your life on your own. These are the consensual human conditions, they are of the first existential and developmental levels, and they always affect your life. Your brotherhood, entourage, or society protect you continuously from unfavorable conditions, yet when these fail, you fail just as well, and you take the blame.

The human conditions follow your life closely in all its elemental details, as birth, marriage, finding a job, and buying a house, determining your fulfillment. Furthermore, the human condition relates directly to the hierarchy of needs, and this is how psychology and sociology define the human condition currently, in this specific relative, empiric manner. We also know that the human condition relates to how humans live their life, as how and what they eat, the type of house they live in, what number of calories they can have a day, or how much time they spend at the gym. Yet there is no relationship among these according to psychology and sociology, and therefore no one seems to know exactly how to define the human condition. Commonly, the human condition is how hard or how easy you have it in life. Yet how exactly can you ever define and measure this?

It seems that people cannot distinguish the human condition from the human life or human lifestyle, or from the human attitudes, or even from the human needs, while the concept of human condition stands well apart from these, with its understanding remaining imperative to the human survival. Because while the human condition remains closely related to the human existence since it is found in the human environment, the human condition opposes the human existence and the human survival while humans fulfill their needs, influencing directly in this manner the human lifestyle. Coincidentally, throughout this book series "Human," I have entire books dedicated to all subjects mentioned above, meant to study, define, and explain the human being, life, this world, and the meaning and condition that humans have in life and in this world.

Why would you ever account for your condition throughout life? Why would you ever bother to know your own human condition? Because, since conditions influence directly your survival, subsistence, development, and existence, many times in your detriment, it is imperative that you remain aware of them throughout life, in order to be capable to identify, predict, and overcome them at any time. Because all it takes is one simple unfavorable condition that you fail to overcome, and it does not matter how successful you had been, because that simple condition marks the end of your existence, or the end of your family existence, the end of your genetic line, and even the end of humanity, and everything is your fault. You can never overcome your own conditions throughout life if you are not capable to understand the concept of the human condition in the first place.

If all these seem so important, then why don't you see everybody taking to the library at once to study all the human conditions closely, or why don't you see the human condition mentioned in the news and throughout the movies? Probably because there would be no bad news anymore for you to watch, if everybody was capable to identify, predict, and cope with all conditions throughout life. Because humans, through their outstanding reasoning, should already be capable to overcome natural and social conditions of up to the third intelligent level and even higher, if they are ever given enough time, knowledge, and resources to prepare. If not, no more you, and no more humanity, because all dreadful conditions overwhelm you, and you go extinct.

As a reference, you find favorable conditions everywhere at

home throughout your casual living, as food in the refrigerator, a roof over your head, a handy thermostat to help you adjust the temperature of your room as you please, or some minor plumbing work in the kitchen that you have to tend to this coming weekend. Second level conditions are harmonious and intuitive, and animals may overcome these continuously through their animal abilities, since animal abilities are of the second level, while obeying the law of the jungle, which is also of the second level. Humans may overcome these second level conditions just as well, highly successfully, overcoming the wild animals just as well, if they ever become a threat and therefore an unfavorable condition. Since security throughout life is one of the major human condition, and it comes at all levels. As a reference, security threats from wild animals are of the second level, matching the second level abilities of all wild animals. Harmony with animals, even with the unfavorable animals, is possible at the third intelligent developmental level and higher.

Third level dreadful conditions may be overcome only by humans, since humans are the only third level intelligent beings on Earth, capable of third level reasoning. This is why you find only humans capable to live throughout ice conditions, throughout deserts, or only on water, as sailors do. These are third level environments of third level conditions, along with living throughout major draughts and throughout other natural calamities. While animals remain incapable and perish throughout these, since animals have only second level intuitive physiological abilities, and second level intuitive thinking.

Conditions do not stop at the third intelligent human level, but they keep augmenting, up to the tenth level. As a reference, the large asteroids that took out dinosaurs sixty million years ago were fourth level dreadful environmental conditions. Explosions and implosions of stars represent fifth level dreadful environmental conditions, if you happen to live in the same stellar system with them.

The human condition does not consist only of bad, unfavorable events, but also of favorable ones, since conditions are good and bad, accounting for all events, details, and characteristics influencing your life. Conditions are good or bad, natural or artificial, harmonious or ordered, natural or consensual, random or predictable, imminent or possible, deliberate or accidental, as it is always important to understand them accordingly, since if you do not, they persist, and many times they amplify, lowering considerably the quality of your life, if they do not take your life altogether. Yet since humans expect a quality of life of the third intelligent level and higher, this might become an issue.

How menacing are these conditions? There are no rules, since everything depends on circumstances, on you, on statistics, and on probability. Because there are people who died throughout first level conditions, as drowning in their own bowl of soup, while others died heroically throughout major wars, tornadoes, and earthquakes just as well, which are third level conditions. Yet since it takes third level conditions and higher to take you down and still be considered a hero, we refer to this as death of the third level. It makes a great difference, because people do not only discriminate your life, but also your death, and you see this in the news.

What conditions can you survive? All of them, certainly, through reasoning, and never through drugs and procrastination. Everybody says so, while doing the opposite. Coping with conditions is more complex and more tedious than it seems. In general, you should always find the most favorable manner to cope with your conditions throughout life. Many times, people use beliefs, tackling unfavorable conditions as the others do, which is be good or bad, depending on circumstances. The availability of food is a major condition throughout life, and this always determines what species die and what carry on. It is not the same with humans, since humans have society to take care of many of their needs, including the need to eat. However, people still act through beliefs in everything relating to their eating conditions, and this leads to the great majority of illnesses and deaths in this world, even to your death, if you are not careful.

Food itself is not the only condition, but the condition is everything related to food. The condition of the food itself is the condition, along with the condition in which you fulfill your need to eat. The food itself is not the only condition, since the condition of the food is the condition, only when this condition, along with all details and characteristics of the food, relate to how you fulfill your need to eat.

How harmful or how harmless is the human condition related to food currently in society? Because all it takes is to fail to cope with only one human unfavorable condition throughout life, and you die, regardless if this was a simple eating or shelter condition. This is why you see people so determined currently to switch to vegetarian diets, to low caloric diets, to low on fat diets, to low on sugar diets, to entirely organic diets, to spend more time at the gym, to spend less time at the gym, to drink more water, or to drink less water, because people are ready to try everything only to improve their health and lifestyle, while these changes cannot help, because most of the assumed problems are not even actual conditions throughout human life. Because some people cannot understand the human condition in all details, but they only do what others do, for no other reason, through consensual beliefs and stereotypes, as this is a human condition in itself.

Are beliefs human conditions in life and in this world? Not only beliefs, but an entire first level consensual ideological underdevelopment, while humans are supposed to be third level intelligent living beings, far above the first consensual ideological servitude level. As you study history and this world, you notice how ideologies harm this world the most, while ideologies influence and control this world the most just as well, because all tyrants found throughout the upper layers of society cannot control and exploit this world without ideologies, jurisdictions, and an entire human addiction, underdevelopment, and consensus.

What can you do? You certainly have to understand human conditions throughout life, and not to assume random conditions as accurate because everybody believes so. People have assumed many types of conditions throughout life, with all irrelevant remedies turning out to be false and harmful, many times with dreadful consequences. This always happens, as it changes your behavior to match the crowd, through irrelevant, harmful activities, while the imminent, important conditions of the intelligent human level remain unidentified, unpredicted, they end up catching you unprepared, and eventually, they harm you badly. This happens to everyone, including your loved ones. Just consider the multitude of people building their homes or buying property on riverbeds, since it is nice to live life by the river. Yet how long will it be before the next time it rains abundantly, causing the river to overflow?

Because you think and you act through beliefs, which are consensual in nature, and therefore you end up doing whatever everyone does. You remain astray, while all those to have implemented these beliefs own a multitude of houses on safe ground all over this world, along with extraordinary underground bunkers just in case the environment switches to fourth level conditions. While they already have enough food and water put aside everywhere, because they are capable to identify and overcome all unfavorable conditions that may ever occur.

What will you do during unfavorable fourth level human conditions? What will you do during normal, unfavorable third level conditions? Because all it takes is to cut off electricity in this world, and you are dead in less than a month depending where you live, while the electric grid is only a first level condition. These people that kept you astray this entire time are capable now to overcome imminent third and fourth level conditions throughout high tech underground shelters, they paid you fifty cents an hour more than the average worker so you can dig the caverns yourself and stock in the provisions, they get to survive now while you die peacefully at home surrounded by your loved ones, yet still happy to have had a job paying you fifty cents an hour more than the average worker. With full benefits. Because it is a belief to assume that the highest values in life relate to money, while beliefs are nothing but first level consensual thinking, lower than the intuitive thinking of wild animals. With this kind of thinking and development, you are expected to survive third and fourth level conditions, which might not happen.

This is why the people of many developed nations die shortly after the authorities cut off the electricity, because with the electricity out and with all goods unavailable, everybody ends up fighting heroically for the last cracker in the grocery store. Everybody becomes the unfavorable human condition of everybody else during significant cataclysms, or not, since it always depends on your developmental level.

Your level of development must match or exceed the level of all your unfavorable conditions in order for you to survive, subsist, prosper, and develop more. Additionally, you have to tend to your environment continuously, to make it favorable and to bring it to your own third intelligent human level, in order to be able to fulfill all your needs at the third intelligent human level in it, otherwise it is impossible to fulfill your human needs, and you end up filling the environment with dreadful conditions instead.

As a reference, your family at home is of the third intelligent human level during the good times, because this is the only intelligent human environment that you have in this world, while you were supposed to have the entire world at the third intelligent human level, because you are an intelligent living human being, and this is what you must always accomplish alongside everybody else, an entire third level intelligent human environment.

At the third intelligent human level, you are supposed to form an entire third level intelligent human environment everywhere, yet instead, you form the first consensual environment that you know well, including the entire unnecessary bureaucracy of Earth. Yet since you can make all tyrants possible only in an ideological bureaucratic manner, you and the entire world remain undeveloped continuously, at the first consensual servitude tyrannical level. This is how you remain decayed, and you cannot predict the unfavorable conditions of the environment as these turn against you, with you unprepared.

Your environmental conditions are the specific environmental details affecting you, positively or negatively. You are already prepared to withstand the unfavorable conditions, through your own knowledge and entire development. Your favorable environmental conditions forming your niche will always help you survive, subsist, prosper, develop, and fulfill your needs and meanings, while your unfavorable conditions stand in your way or harm you, according to their level. The third intelligent level is the human level, while the third level unfavorable conditions are called calamities, and you may withstand them only within your third level intelligent human environment, third level intelligent human society, and third level intelligent human civilization, if you are developed at the third intelligent human level, along with everyone else. Yet if everybody else is undeveloped, you will not make it. You survive third level dreadful environmental conditions only if everything is at the third level in the human society, as genuine equality, prosperity, positive interconnectivity, freedom, genuine education and genuine knowledge, along with an advanced, third level technology. Otherwise, you go extinct, mostly since the current society is of the first consensual, made only for corporations and for the entire bureaucracy of Earth, not for living human beings.

The third level intelligent human society stated here is nowhere in this world, because it is erased continuously by the first level consensual enslaved tyrannical human society that you find everywhere. The third level intelligent human society is part of the third level intelligent human environment that is actually erased continuously, in order to make servitude and tyranny possible, in order for all tyrants to have someone to make their beds, polish their shoes, pour their drinks, and wash their clothes. Yet since you can have drugs only in an undeveloped world, everybody loves this world, and therefore everybody erases continuously the third level intelligent human environment, with the third level intelligent human society included. There might be exploding stars and falling meteorites throughout the good movies, yet those never harm this world, because these only kill dinosaurs, while the dinosaurs died long ago and do not matter anymore. How could you ever stop taking drugs for this nonsense?

In an intelligent human society, you do not even have to go through third level unfavorable conditions or lower, since these are avoided or overcome directly, without affecting society and anyone within. Because this is why intelligent living beings live life within developed societies and civilizations, because these are capable to assure their comprehensive fulfillment by protecting them from all unfavorable conditions up to their own level, and by assuring them the favorable conditions up to their own level. Yet the current human society is not genuinely developed at the third intelligent human level, but it is only consensual, of the first servitude tyrannical level.

This means that the current human society is capable to protect you from unfavorable conditions up to the first level, which are basic floods, riots, financial bankruptcy, fluctuations in the price of rice, and terminal illnesses, while assuring you all the necessary favorable conditions up to the first level. This is why unfavorable second level conditions affect you, as famines, pandemics, and even floods, as you see in the news, while you never have assured the fulfillment of your basic needs as your food and shelter, but you have to go to work all day to assure these yourself, at this first level, in a consensual manner. This is how, currently, the human society can barely survive the normal second level unfavorable conditions.

Considering the favorable environmental conditions by level, the third level favorable human conditions are mandatory for a favorable intelligent human life, development, and fulfillment, while the second level favorable environmental conditions assure a normal subsistence, as having food, water, and proper temperature at home. It is worse when the higher level reliable favorable environmental or social conditions turn around to become unfavorable conditions, at the same third level, because this is how your entire human existence is menaced, which happens often in the Consensual Matrix.

Why exactly having this confusion with these levels of conditions, similar in number but different when they are favorable and unfavorable? Why can't we just make a clearer, more reliable model of the human condition? This is the only model, the only manner to model conditions even at the intelligent human level, because your comprehensive condition is made naturally in this manner, through normal interconnectivity, because many times, the environment is limited in its details, as in its food, water, money, land, opportunities, social status, workforce, privileges, and income. This means that, in a limited world, through limited resources, everything favoring you can become unfavorable to others through you and through your own interconnectivity in this world, because in order for you to have more, others must have less or nothing at all. Because for all limited favorable conditions, once you lack them, they become unfavorable conditions but at the same level, taking you down if you are not careful.

Are you happy now with your university degree, new car, excellent job, beautiful wife, and a lovely neighborhood, which are third level achievements that you have made recently since you have joined the Lower Brotherhood? Be very careful, because once the Brotherhood disfavors you, they turn around to become unfavorable conditions just by losing them. Even then, you never know if you can go through the tedious bankruptcy, unemployment, and divorce procedures coming at their third unfavorable level, with you now back in the Masses, broke, discouraged, and finished, since this is the current consensual masonry of Earth, deliberately. Consensual human conditions constrain you continuously to serve at your best, deliberately, and many times, you do so regardless of what you become in this world, good condition or dreadful condition. Because Brothers are made to harm you for various reasons, many times only to constrain you to serve better or only as a warning, for various personal agendas, or for your refusal to harm others, as you have to consider these as human conditions just as well, throughout your entire social interaction. This is always the case in an undeveloped world, while throughout undeveloped consensual worlds, everything is maintained in this musical chairs manner, in order to enhance servitude and in order to make all tyrants possible.

Yet this is the case only if you are more developed, since when you are developed at the intelligent human level, you cannot harm others, you seek equality and prosperity in the world, and furthermore, you seek to use your entire influence within the Brotherhood to make a better world, while interfering in this manner with the entire system of exploitation of Earth, making all tyrants mad. Abundance, development, social equality, prosperity, justice, and intelligent harmony are excellent conditions for the entire world, yet once you interfere with the entire system of exploitation of Earth, they remove you from the Brotherhood, while making an example of you.

In contrast, at a lower developmental level, you are willing to do everything just as told in a consensual society, regardless if you harm this world or not, as you see it everywhere. Currently, the more the people are underdeveloped, the more the Brotherhood thrives. Because once you have fifty cents an hour more than the average worker, you are happy to do anything in life for all your authorities, regardless of consequences.

Why should be anything wrong with this, mostly when it is the case with the majority of people? Because there is a specific characteristic of intelligent human beings called human responsibility, and that filters out harmful, irrelevant, unnecessary activities before you even undergo them. Human responsibility would have stopped you to build underground shelters for the very rich while knowing that the rest of the world will perish at the surface. More precisely, while knowing that instead of investing all that time, effort, and knowledge in building your own shelter, you build it for others, for those to have controlled you continuously, for them to survive now, and for fifty cents an hour that they give you for them to live and for you and your loved ones to die. Look around, to see how everybody else would do the same, the entire Brotherhood. Human responsibility is referred to as human care in the current masonry, and thy burn it during ceremonies, for you to destroy the world.

Why lacking human responsibility? Humans are never born at the intelligent human level, but it is only through their lifelong education, training, and continuous learning that humans manage to achieve their intelligent human developmental level, or this is the case if they ever get there, since humans tend to remain astray and underdeveloped on lower levels, while they enjoy drugs, entertainment, dogma, irrelevant wars, and tempting servitude throughout the multitude of hierarchies. Humans love harming the world, while humans love drugs instead. This is how people live their life at the zero level throughout major sicknesses and addictions, at the first level throughout brotherhoods, military, and tight careers, or at the second level through animal instincts and reflexes, never at the intelligent human level.

This is how you have to live your life below the human level, because you have no choice, since society will always drag you down. If you personalize your lifestyle in any manner, all those around will find you different and will target you just because they can, only to switch you back to match the crowd. This is a harmful human condition in itself, because those on top of society that claim to take care of you, if you only hand in your authority to them, design and impose your current lifestyle consensual and addicted, and it is always done against you. Societies are supposed to be of the third intelligent level, offering you the favorable conditions matching your third level human nature, since this is how Life made you. Therefore, you cannot fulfill Life at the third intelligent human level as she demands, since you lack the means, will, environment, knowledge, abilities, development, and proper interconnectivity at the same third intelligent human level. The current consensual society functions inadequately, forcing larger unfavorable conditions on you. While you can never pinpoint exactly what goes on in your life, only that you tend to feel sick, depressed, meaningless, and unfulfilled continuously, probably from drinking and smoking too much, while you are constantly broke, because you always lose your job and it is always your fault, your inability, with your spouse divorcing you in the middle of all these, and taking the children. This happens job after job and spouse after spouse, so yes, it must be your fault. Yet you can never advance the level of your thinking to see everything from above, to see your real harmful conditions destroying your life repeatedly, to see that these are artificial, consensual in nature, and they are caused deliberately by society, in every manner, after the most pertinent public relators consecrate their lives to design them and to implement them in this world. These are artificial third level unfavorable social conditions, fed continuously to people that think at the first and second levels. What chance can you ever have to survive? None, since all these third level dreadful, enforced social conditions targeting you are similar to major third level natural disasters, only that you are targeted in society for life not only occasionally, at the same dreadful third environmental level. This is the case if you are in the Masses and the Lower Brotherhood.

We keep finding this specific theme everywhere: authorities claim to act on your behalf while they always go against you if you are from the lower social layers and from the wrong genetic lines, leaving you and your loved ones to die throughout famines, wars, and natural calamities, while blaming your loss on faith, probability, statistics, and on your own laziness, ignorance, and sin.

These problems never happen to them, as they consider themselves superior. Since you can identify the main actors, study closely the kind of society that they shape and reshape in this world for you, to find everything working against you, causing people to work, act, compete, and fight one against another only to be able to fulfill basic needs for subsistence, and therefore rendering them underdeveloped, meaningless, unfulfilled, and astray throughout life and throughout the world. Society does not help you to overcome your dreadful conditions as all politicians promise, but society itself becomes an unfavorable condition, with you having to reason and work at your best only to be able to overcome it, with no time left for you to develop and maintain yourself at the intelligent human level. Because otherwise, none of those tyrants found throughout the upper layers of society would be possible.

You understand why everybody remains ignorant of the concept of human condition throughout life, among other concepts as the human development, human rights, human existence, human meaning, human status, human fulfillment, human lifestyle, and human stereotypes, since it is meant to be in this manner, in order for you to remain astray and underdeveloped throughout life, while still unprepared for any imminent higher level unfavorable condition ever coming your way. Since once it comes, you are gone, discarded by Life first, and if you still make it, discarded by the current consensual society.

While having to cope with your conditions, you also have to compete with everyone for survival, since you are in this world together, rich and poor alike. Yet with you already disabled, incapable, weak, and unprepared, you are the first one to fail and to clear the way, to let those controlling you take over this world and keep it for themselves. Because you might consider major calamities only once a year, while watching horror movies, because they are this much ridiculed and ignored. While those controlling society are already competing with you by now, before the major calamity starts, so what chance do you have? If it takes too long for the major calamity to come, then they provoke it themselves, by unleashing artificial third level unfavorable conditions throughout society. As they have already tried to do with ebola in Africa and covid throughout the world, or as they try to start a major war around Europe, which everybody else tries to avoid, and life goes on, one major deliberate dreadful human condition after another, dark age after dark age. Yet once you give people drugs, they love you dearly, as tyrannical as you are.

You may always claim that this is too pessimistic, and the probability of your survival in this world can never be so low, yet look throughout this world and throughout history, to find out how low your life may get, because nobody is privileged in this world. Only those capable to predict their unfavorable conditions well ahead have a chance in life, with the rest becoming simple statistics, data worth mentioning throughout the evening news.

Just assess your means, and abilities. Can you withstand third and fourth level unfavorable natural and social conditions? What would you do once they manifest? How would you gather all your loved ones around in order to protect them or to protect each other? Where would you go? How would you fulfill your needs? How well will you manage to remain in control? Would you trust the authorities? Because many times throughout history and throughout the world, authorities send their people straight to concentration camps, working camps, unnecessary wars, hospitals, and morgues. Would you fight against others because your ideology tells you to do so? Because you might do so, you might be willing to harm anyone for your ideologies. Because ideologies are based on beliefs and not on intelligent reasoning, and through beliefs, you make anyone do anything in life, even harm and kill others, on your behalf, since this makes all tyrants possible. You have them at the lodge.

What can you do? Develop, stay out of drugs, prepare, and if your authorities ever harm people or let them down in any circumstance, then they certainly do the same to you and your loved ones, even if you are in the Middle Brotherhood. Be ready and prepared by now to have to overcome your major unfavorable conditions on your own, without their help. How will you behave throughout the next war or cataclysm? Just be prepared. Where exactly will your family meet when it happens? What will you carry with you? Will you leave loved ones behind if they fail to show up, only to save the rest? Where will you go from there? How will you stay in touch after all conventional means of communication fail? How will you cope with security threats?

If you find these irrelevant, if you find them worthy to be postponed for the following day or for the following weekend, then you may do so, because all major cataclysms can always wait, since none took place during your lifetime. Why exactly should they happen currently or this week? Isn't it better to pour another drink and watch the media quietly, without cataclysms?

Because you are made deliberately to take your drugs and watch the media, only to remain astray and unprepared. Major calamities do not happen too often, so you may not have the chance to go through them, despite of how stressful, dreadful, and tedious it may seem. Who would ever want to be in any of these circumstances? You, certainly. What kind of videogames are very appealing to you and to everybody else? All videogames relate to major wars and dreadful cataclysms, as terrible as these can be, when you always have to survive under the most dreadful conditions and circumstances, and people love it. Everybody. What exactly do their souls seek in this world? A nice, peaceful life, or a lifetime of drugs and totalitarian oppression? The name of this game is "Terra," from terror and terrible.

We study not only dreadful conditions, but also benefic ones, when your main task is not to survive through them, but to do anything in order to identify and use them on your behalf, as quickly and efficiently as possible. Even throughout major dreadful conditions, these smaller, less obvious favorable conditions manifest continuously and are capable to save your life and the lives of your loved ones, or this is the case if you are capable to identify them and make use of them immediately, since Existence itself is made of good and bad elements, many times simultaneously.

What exactly are conditions? You already know your natural and social environments, and how to cope, survive, and prosper in them. Conditions are everything standing and acting independently of you in life and in this world, independently of your reasoning, ability, behavior, and lifetime activity. Everything that you cannot control directly and unconditionally remains a condition for you throughout life and throughout the world, including all vices and all desires of your loved ones, with your spouse and cat included, while many times, your conditions include your spouse and your cat entirely.

Because you cannot control living beings and intelligences rigidly, by default, but you have to act and behave alongside them, with them as conditions in your life and in your world. Yet since it is the same with them, and since they depend on you as much as you depend on them, you know better, and you form the harmony together, remaining good conditions one for another.

It is the same while driving, since all obstacles and vehicles in the road are your conditions, with everybody seeking to remain a good condition for you, or at least a neutral condition. Road rage is different, since you make yourself a dreadful condition on the road deliberately, for various purposes.

It is the same in society, because you can always be a dreadful or a benefic social condition to those around, since it depends. If you break the social harmony, the others take revenge or they take you out altogether. Yet they always break the harmony with you, and they never care, or it pleases them. Many times, their ideologies constrain them to behave against you and against themselves. If you are not of their nation, color, faction, social class, wealth level, status, power, ideology, jurisdiction, race, continent, city, genetic line, region, age, gender, sect, crest, or cult, they keep you down, they exploit you, or they take you out, even consensually.

Consensus means agreement, the particular agreement that they keep implemented against you. This might seem exaggerated, yet you must always consider that in the current undeveloped addicted exploitive world, the entire society is not with you, but it is always in competition against you. It is called social competition, and it is even encouraged by the capitalist social ideology. If you manage to have around yourself a small social cushion of loved ones and very good friends, keep it as much as you can, because it is a rarity in this undeveloped world. This might be your only third level intelligent human social environment that you will ever have. Otherwise, with no one alongside you, you will always be a target in the current consensual world, because this is the current human social condition, always in competition against you.

You might want to identify all conditions of your life and existence, to understand their purpose, origin, and manifestation, while understanding your behavior related to them, predicting and preparing for them well in advance. For benefic conditions, you want to identify them, preserve them, and use them in a harmonious efficient manner.

You might be tempted to associate the worst with all conditions, good and bad, yet this is never the case. Life never has bad intentions or major failures in any of her plans and meanings throughout your life, and this includes conditions, as dreadful as these might seem. There is always a meaning for everything in your life, and this always seems to be cognitive and developmental in nature, for you or for your community, society, or for the entire world. When you study your lifetime conditions closely, you find them not random, not void of meaning, but alive and meaningful, since your entire life is not actually your continuous fight for survival as science might state, but it is always life interconnected with life at all classes and levels for the same subsistence, for the same fulfillment, and for the same existential niches. This is the case in nature, in society, and everywhere throughout your life. Normal people and normal living beings in general are always your conditions, and therefore this adds to your choices of how to cope throughout life, because you may fight continuously throughout life as in a major cataclysm if you ever decide to live your life in this manner, or you may work hard to instate and keep instated a benefic harmony engulfing you and those around throughout all interactions that you may undergo throughout life.

Even significant unfavorable conditions may become favorable to you, if you ever know how to turn them around, because these will always help you develop significantly, if you only bother to involve your developmental effort in order to learn and strengthen yourself through them. Furthermore, you can always pay others to cope with your own problems, as it is done everywhere throughout society, yet expect these people to train and develop in your place, while you pay them to do so, with you also having to depend on them from then on, throughout all similar circumstances. Because self-reliance means freedom to fulfill needs and meanings, assuring your continuous fulfillment and development.

Let us model your natural conditions, since natural conditions always seem to interact with Life more than social classes and entire societies. This might not be the case with humans, since humans live life within societies, which have their own consensual conditions and environments. We study social conditions in another chapter, but let us study first natural conditions as these influence living beings in general, and as these influence human beings in particular.

2 NATURAL CONDITIONS OF THE NATURAL ENVIRONMENT

Throughout this study of the human conditions, and throughout all studies of this book series "Human," you want to find the idea, the meaning, and the reasoning behind each mental model of each book. Because I do not give you a specific list of what you have to do throughout life in order to be able to avoid all bad conditions, while accepting only the favorable ones, since any list of what you must do in life becomes your list of laws, rules, regulations, chores, and beliefs, with entire sets of these laws and beliefs becoming ideologies and jurisdictions. While this world is full of these, as each ideology and jurisdiction is used to control as many people as possible. I usually determine you to learn, study, develop, reason continuously, and reason independently, while avoiding beliefs, drugs, additives, servitude, and control, to live your life at the intelligent human level. While you may do so or not, since it is your choice how you live your life.

In the natural environment, it is not too difficult to see how species develop and adapt. Yet species do not have to adapt to the entire environment, but only to one specific niche of the environment. Niches are specific sets of favorable environmental elements and conditions, as eating grass, being capable to live in hot or cold temperatures, living inside forests or out in the open, or living in the water or on land. If you are a carnivore, grass is not exactly part of your own niche, so you do not have to worry about it throughout life. What you worry about is to have enough food to eat, and how to remain capable to hunt it. It is the same with herbivores, since what these are interested in is to reach grassy lands, and to protect themselves from predators. This is why herbivores gather in herds, because grass in general is abundant, allowing them to live together.

Within herds, you still have the chance to survive predators, if you are only faster and more capable than those around, so predators catch the others first. While predators have to be strong and healthy themselves, only to be able to catch their prey, since the prey becomes faster and more capable to escape them with each generation.

However, this is only a first level algorithmic mechanical explanation of the environment and its conditions, while life is different, starting with the second intuitive level, not with the first algorithmic mechanical level. Automatic mechanisms are not considered alive, but only objects, while life starts with the second intuitive level characterizing all wild animals on Earth. Therefore, predators do not become stronger to continuously in order to be able to reach the fastest antelope on Earth to eat it. Live in general does not develop in order to reach the highest niche, but life develops in order to maintain harmony in every manner while fulfilling its needs and meanings in the most lively harmonious efficient manner, which is significantly better than becoming only stronger or only smarter. You might not be able to grasp the meaning of harmony and harmonious conditions of any environment, because the current human environment is never harmonious, but always consensual, drastic, and radical, and this is why you tend to understand all animal environments and all animal conditions similar to the current human environment and to the human conditions, which are consensual entirely, of the first consensual and algorithmic level, which is the level of ideologies, hierarchies, and automatic mechanisms.

The human laws are always algorithmic, mechanical, ideological, and always consensual, making you assume that everything in life and in the world must be algorithmic, mechanical, ideological, and consensual, yet this is never the case in life. This is why the current consensual biology, zoology, and anatomy studies everything in a mechanical manner, with hearts considered pumps and stomachs considered chemical plants, which is not the case. Everything is alive within cells, organisms, and in the outside world in all natural environments, while only humans are mechanical, ideological, tyrannical, and consensual, because humans are considered corporations, not living human beings, while corporations can always be exploited even in a tyrannical abusive manner, because all corporations are similar, and therefore they are replaceable and disposable. The dreadful law of the jungle as depicted by science is found only among undeveloped humans, and only in the current consensual society, not in Nature, because Nature is not of the first automatic consensual level, but Nature starts with the second intuitive living level, which is always harmonious. You even lose your niche in Nature and in Life if you are not meaningful, harmonious, careful, preserving, and fulfilling.

The law of the jungle itself is not of the first survival algorithmic mechanical level, with lions eating antelopes every time when they are capable to catch them, and every time when they are hungry, since this is not exactly the case in the jungle. Carnivores are always careful not to harm their niche, otherwise they go extinct, while in this manner they always maintain harmony with their niche. Only human hunters shoot and catch everything that they can, with the largest specimens considered an honor and a virtue among human hunters, which is the normal first careless ideological consensual level, ruining the world.

In Nature, in wilderness, and everywhere else in Life, living beings do not use their niche randomly, exploitably, and abusively, because this is only the first consensual tyrannical level, characteristic only to undeveloped human beings. All living beings use their niche in the most harmonious careful manner, in order to preserve them for as long as possible, because without their niche, they go extinct.

Study closely all food chains, which are the most delicate niche on Earth, to see how all living beings preserve them in the most harmonious adequate manner in order to have them for as long as possible, otherwise they go extinct. Study the jungle closely, in order to notice its actual law, because it is never ideological, careless, exploitive, tyrannical, and consensual as it is the case in the human society, but it is always harmonious, with all carnivores preserving their prey as much as possible, even in a harmonious manner.

Carnivores do not eat all animals at once just because they can catch them, but they eat only the old, the sick, the dying, and the disabled, because these cannot reproduce, and cannot replenish their niche. Study all carnivores closely in the wilderness, to see how they tend to all herds closely, always protecting them and always caring for them, even when they are very hungry, because they must maintain their number large, assuring an abundant niche on a longer term, because only in this manner, they can assure their own family to remain strong, numerous, and very capable.

All lions eat only the sick antelopes, the old, and those who cannot reproduce, identifying them through smell, and chasing them throughout the herd to eat only them, never eating the healthy animals who can still reproduce. This is the actual law of the jungle, always harmonious at the second intuitive level, never mechanical, abusive, careless, and tyrannical at the first consensual algorithmic level as it is the case currently with humans.

This determines closely the entire development of life on Earth, and not the theory of evolution with its survival of the fittest. Study closely the theory of evolution and the survival of the fittest, to see how they explain life and the development of life in a mechanical random manner, never in a living intuitive intelligent harmonious manner as it is the case in the real world ever since the dawn of life. The current science states that predators become stronger to reach their prey while the prey become stronger in order to escape predators, while this is only a mechanical algorithmic explanation of the first level, below the levels of life, while all life always develops in an intuitive intelligent harmonious careful preserving manner continuously.

How does development happen? Subjectively and cognitively, through intelligences, since these develop and specialize throughout their subjective life according to all existential niches and according to all specific conditions of these existential niches, always in a harmonious, intuitive intelligent careful preserving manner. All intelligences live life together by the zillions in a harmonious specialized meaningful fulfilling manner, never working one against another, while they maintain this continuous living harmonious fulfilling interconnectivity within cells and organisms, and in the outside world in all environments.

Study closely your cellular components, cells, tissue, organs, and bodily systems, to see how they are always meaningful, harmonious, fulfilling, and successful, never working one against another, while always fulfilling all tasks within cells and within the organism flawlessly. While if there is ever a problem within the organism and in the outside world, it is mostly your fault as a conscious intelligence, because you tend to apply the same carelessness, selfishness, meaningless, and lack of harmony that you apply in the outside world, because this is how all humans behave in the outside world, at the zero addicted level or at the first consensual mechanical careless tyrannical level.

The current consensual society does not even consider cells and cellular components alive, while never considering intelligences alive, by ignoring the living intelligences altogether, while explaining everything in a mechanical consensual ideological manner. However, the current consensual society is part of the Consensual Matrix and is never allowed to consider and to address anything alive, but only the consensual, never the real, and never the alive. This is how all humans are considered corporations, since the current consensual society is made only for corporations. Study closely the entire bureaucracy and politics of Earth, to see how they never address living human beings, but only corporations and jurisdictions. The entire current consensual masonry is not even made for living human beings, as it was the case with the old masonry of Earth that lasted for entire golden ages with the freemasons and rosicrucians included, but for exploitation, as it is integral part of the Consensual Matrix, making possible the entire human exploitation in the West.

Apart from the consensual society, there is the living intelligent human society, which is currently neglected and ignored. Only at home in the family during the good times you are capable to instate the living intelligent human society, which is the actual living intelligent human family, but only during the good times, when addictions and ideologies are kept out.

Existence is composed of existential niches for all living beings, and this is why you have entire environments, natural environments or class environments, being composed of niches themselves. Throughout this study, we have to consider simultaneously life, intelligence, physical bodies, and existence, since these are interconnected, as simple projections or perspectives of the same thing.

For example, you are not only alive, you are not only intelligent, and you are not only your physical body, because you cannot be these separately. Because life, intelligence, and physical body are three correspondences of a same oneness, while you are always these three simultaneously. You are an entire lifeline of existence containing your mind, body, and soul, and more. Everything in this world is alive, intelligent, and exists objectively through a physical body, and this includes any living being and object in this world, since you may find life everywhere, in all forms of life, not only organic, and in all realities, not only in this world.

At the supreme level, Life, Intelligence, and the wider world are similar correspondences of each other. This world is alive and intelligent entirely. Therefore, while studying living beings as they cope with the conditions of their environment, you have to study all three correspondences simultaneously: life, intelligence, and physical body, since all these cope and are influenced throughout this developmental process.

If you study only the physical body, because it is easier to observe throughout the ages, and therefore it easier to explain empirically, then you end up with worthless theories as the theory of evolution, while science is full of these empiric, erroneous scientific speculations, theories, and beliefs. This keeps you underdeveloped, because you lack the necessary accurate knowledge helping you live your life at the third intelligent human level. This creates larger and larger unfavorable conditions throughout life, through the incapability and unwillingness of science to create and release in society the advanced technology necessary for an intelligent human society, as free of cost energy, free transportation, and automatic processing plants. Because by having these, humans are able to live life without currencies and without authorities, while authorities currently exploit, harass, and kill this world systematically.

Why do authorities do so? Those controlling authorities compete offensively with you and with the rest of this world, because you have the same resources, niches, environments, and conditions together in this world, regardless of the species or society you are in. Therefore, in an undeveloped consensual world, you do not have care, harmony, and fulfillment, but you have only competition throughout life, regardless if you are poor or rich. The only difference is your developmental level, because if you happen to be higher in development, you are capable to engage in harmonious interactions with those around, while if you are at a lower developmental level, you engage in the well-known tyrannical win-lose interaction, because you must be a tyrant in order to win at the expense of others in the common win-lose interaction.

It is as eating the food of your children at the dinner table in order for you to have more, in the common win-lose interaction that you know well from the current consensual society. Yet you never do so at the dinner table, because the human family is the last patch of living intelligent human society left in this undeveloped world, with all family members placing themselves only in win-win harmonious interconnectivities, or even in lose-win circumstances, if they are not capable to fulfill all needs of all family members, because children are always prioritized if this ever happens. We find these lose-win circumstances even in the jungle, because all jungle is alive.

Whenever biology teaches you at school that humans are animals, it must refer to these underdeveloped human beings, because they behave as animals. How can you tell the difference? If people fulfill throughout life only second level animal needs as eating, sleeping, reproduction, breathing, or security and social needs, then they are animals, since they live life at the animal level. If you still cannot find anything else to do in life besides fulfilling these animal needs, if you cannot identify intelligent human needs, then you should focus more human intelligence, intelligent human interconnectivity, and intelligent human harmony.

The second animal intuitive level is still a high developmental level in the current consensual society, since most of the people live life at the first consensual level, in servitude or in tyranny, throughout the tight hierarchies of society, or they live life at the zero addicted level, as the very sick, the disabled, and the addicted. If you study the people around you closely, and if you find them all taking drugs, even only coffee, beer, hemp, pills, medication, and wine, this is the zero addicted level, reaching everybody, the entire humanity, to the point where all souls come here for tyranny, terror, irrelevance, and drugs, marking the most dreadful human condition in this world.

Your conditions are not only the food, security, and shelter that you must provide, but the type of food, security, and shelter that you can have. Your significant condition as an herbivore is the type of predators that you have around, because the less dangerous they are, the better it is for you. However, as an entire species or as an entire kingdom, the food itself may be a condition for you as well, because niches change from individuals to the entire race, to the entire species, and to the entire class.

Niches also change throughout time, they even move around the continent throughout climatic changes, while entire species of plants and animals follow them closely. If you notice the climate changing decade by decade, then expect niches to move around at the same rate, and expect all species to follow them around just as well. There are not invasive species, but only ignorant people interfering with the plant and animal life as it moves around the continent while following its niche.

Therefore, throughout major climatic changes, expect tropical species to find their way to Florida, as exotic lizards and exotic birds already do. Authorities might define these as invasive species, calling for their extermination, yet these are not invasive species, since species never invade new territories, but they only follow their niches around, wherever these take them.

By interfering with their freedom to reach their niches, they go extinct, since humans are always the major dreadful condition for all species of plants and animals on Earth. Humans are the most dreadful condition for humans just as well, to the point where humans themselves render humanity extinct. It was not supposed to be in this manner in a human world, only that the current society is consensual, as it is not a human world or human environment as the politicians imply.

Species are always capable to adapt to changes in their environment whenever other species fail. When you study adaptation closely, you notice that it is not exactly an adaptation to the environment, but it is an entire development, allowing species the possibility to accept new elements within their old niche, or allowing species the possibility to take over neighboring niches, if these happen to become vacant for any reason, as the extinction of the specific species to have occupied them until then.

What we see on Earth is the continuous invasion and migration of humans from their own original niche, to cover almost all niches of the natural environment of Earth. This is what societies allow, a rapid and certain expansion to cover all niches of an entire environment, because humans and developed societies in general are capable to change the environment entirely on their favor, one niche after another, bringing them in the human niche. While with these niches occupied, now their original species have to go extinct. Yet if they are more capable, they move around and they occupy other niches, stealing away from other species, then those other, less capable species go extinct, and these invading species survive. This is lack of harmony, and it happens only with humans, but only with the humans kept undeveloped, meaningless, and unharmonious in life and in the world, while ruining life and the world.

Yet there are still free niches left on Earth for species to inhabit freely. Furthermore, the human existence on Earth has made available new niches everywhere around humans, with plant and animal species rushing in to occupy them even if they have to live life at a very close proximity with humans, which is the case with the species that humans call pests.

Because it is never a survival of the fittest taking place throughout evolution and throughout the ages, with death and extinction taking down and filtering out all those incapable to adapt and survive, but it is always a matter of being capable to develop, morph, change, better yourself, and develop in all domains, in order to be able to follow your niche around wherever it takes you, and to be able to accommodate your own niche whenever invasive species come to occupy it. Yet as you study animals closely, you notice how they go extinct if their niche expires, never taking from other species, but letting them live. You even find multiple species on the same niche, always living life in harmony, while they could have exterminated the other species in order for them to have the entire niche, yet they never do so.

Why not? Why not taking the entire niche and the entire Earth for yourself as any animal or plant species? The niches themselves are very complex, because they are also alive, part of life, while life is very complex. Life never monopolizes niches, because it would decrease efficiency and living harmony, but life maximizes the use of all niches in any manner possible, even by having one species on top of another on top of another as it is the case with the food chains. The entire harmony of life might seem awkward for you if you live your life only at the first consensual level, because you must be developed at the third intelligent level to understand everything.

Life always maximizes, harmonizes, cares for, and preserves all its niches in order to have more, in order to subsist and develop, and in order not to go extinct. Life achieves this entire harmony in all its environmental conditions including its favorable conditions called niches because life is not lived only at the physical objective level, but also at the cognitive intelligence level. Your intelligences send you all your needs and meanings, and this is what you fulfill continuously, your needs and meanings, according to all you feelings, good and bad, exactly as your intelligences send them to you. The physical bodies hold, maintain, fulfill, and develop their own intelligences, yet the intelligences themselves are more fulfilling to themselves and to all systems of intelligences that they form above than to their physical bodies. In this manner, all intelligences including the human intelligences are more meaningful and more fulfilling to themselves and to all systems of intelligences that they form together from the base up, all the way up to Life herself. All intelligences are more fulfilling to Life than they are to their own physical bodies, because only in this manner, they are capable to maintain the entire fulfilling harmony among themselves, to the point where no intelligence works against another.

How exactly do species evolve? How exactly do humans evolve? Because science has never been able to offer a fulfilling explanation, besides the erroneous, empiric, superficial, trivial theory of evolution, which fits well in a short sentence: the fittest survives and the unfit dies. This is as claiming that the big fish eats the little fish because it is bigger and therefore it survives, while the little fish does not survive and goes extinct, in the stomach of the big fish. Even little children know this, since this is what evolution teaches. Science always offers incompetent theories and theorems. The people cannot find their own accurate knowledge, because science monopolizes this world in what it concerns science and knowledge in general. Alternative theories are still available, you may find them over the Internet yet nobody is interested, since they are worse than the mainstream. Yet no one seems to care, because everybody takes drugs, making everybody incapable to differentiate between the accurate and the fake.

How do living beings and species in general evolve? Because we see them developing, changing, and morphing throughout time, with better, more capable, more adapted species replacing the old ones. Evolution is a consensual ideological term, and I use development instead, which is alive. Similarly, harmony is a living term, different from equality, which is more algorithmic, of the first level.

Living beings and species in general develop continuously, in order to be able to cope with the continuous change of their environment, of their niches, and of their conditions, as these change continuously. As a species and as a living being, you also have to change and to develop continuously, alongside everybody else, to match your continuously changing conditions. If not, you are not capable to fulfill your needs, and you die. Yet since the environment itself is alive, in all its favorable and unfavorable conditions, and since all life develops altogether harmoniously, it is not exactly a continuous struggle for survival as the current science depicts, but it is a comprehensive harmonious development, undergone continuously by Life, and you cannot study only one living being or only one species in order to understand the entire development of Life.

Many times, this entire comprehensive living development

matches all astronomical conditions, yet as you study all space objects closely, you find them always alive, even if they are of a different type of life or of different forms of life. Life might be of the same electromagnetic type in stars, yet throughout stars, the electromagnetic type of life has different forms of life above the ionic form of life from stars, which are more difficult to identify, yet they are similarly intuitive and intelligent as the life on Earth. The life of all stars makes possible all heat that they radiate to make life on Earth and on other planets possible, while through all heat variations, you have all climatic changes of Earth, causing all species to migrate or to develop altogether in order to be able to maintain their niche.

All development of life is comprehensive, involving all life of all types and forms, on all planets, stars, and in the interstellar space. You cannot isolate only one form of life, only one species, or only one living being in order to study and explain the development of life, because life and the development of life are comprehensive, and you must study everything in order to understand everything, all environments, all niches, all living beings, all species, all forms of life, all types of life, all space objects, all realities, and the entire wider world. Yet this is only the physical perspective, at the objective, physical, material level, while you must study all intelligences involved, along with their continuous harmonious interconnectivity that they always achieve while fulfilling all their specialized tasks within cellular components, cells, organisms, societies, nations, species, ecosystems, realities, and cluster of realities, up to Life, Intelligence, and the wider world themselves. While in this entire living meaningful harmonious fulfilling comprehensive achievement, here comes science with its theory of evolution to state that the capable species evolve while the incapable die away extinct because they are not fit, this is what all life is, and this is how all life evolves.

How do living beings develop and adapt to their changing environment? Through what exact procedures? How do living beings and entire species know even before they start developing how the environment will look like in the future, for them to end up matching exactly their environment with their own development ages later, and therefore being capable to cope with it exactly as it becomes? The theory of evolution answers trivially: because if they do not match their environment in the future with their development, then they go extinct. Yet since the surviving species are still around, this means that they were evolved enough to cope with the environment.

This does not answer the question. The question is how exactly species evolve, while the theory of evolution explains why evolved species do not go extinct. This might be an accurate answer despite of its triviality, but it is the answer for a different question, making the entire theory of evolution inadequate and therefore worthless. It is as stating that hot water is hot, heavy objects are heavy, and straight lines are straight because they are not curved. Species evolve because they do not go extinct, since this is what the theory of evolution teaches, in a rather trivial, ignorant, inadequate, irrelevant manner. Who are these people?

Then, what exactly is the theory of evolution capable to explain? Why is the entire world so found of it? What exactly is science capable to explain? Why is the entire world so found of the current consensual science? The entire world is controlled to behave in this manner, through strong beliefs, social stereotypes, and indoctrination. While the theory of evolution contains a classification of many species, and this is pertinent. Yet classification is not evolution, which means that this is an entirely different topic of subject replacing another, while answering different questions altogether, while calling itself a theory or a speculation, which means that it is not accurate, neither reliable, nor true, stated even officially, because it is called theory, by the people implementing it in this world, as a theory, assumption, or speculation.

What exactly is going on in this world, and what kind of unfavorable condition is this? It is a consensual condition, as you may find many of these posing as natural and even as favorable human conditions. While they are meant to harm this world, at least by keeping it underdeveloped, which is a major unfavorable human condition.

Why exactly do you find this misleading knowledge exactly for topics studying the nature and meaning of this world, of humanity, and of all human beings? Because this knowledge is concealed the most. I study knowledge, intelligence, life, accuracy, cognition, interconnectivity, reasoning, society, consensus, addictions, servitude, tyranny, achievement, humanity, behavior, meaning, development, and fulfillment throughout this entire book series "Human," and it takes dozens of books to cover everything, because the mainstream and alternative science never help, hiding everything.

Without the proper, accurate human knowledge in this world, you have to keep around a major unfavorable human condition related to human lack of development and human lack of fulfillment, rendering humans extinct, while nobody is willing to learn anything important, while ignoring everything deliberately, focusing only on drugs, tyranny, and social superiority.

How exactly do snakes and antelopes know how to morph their bodies in order to become exactly what they are currently, being able simultaneously to fit the specific niche that they occupy currently? This is as asking how exactly the bottom of the puddle can match so perfectly the hole in the road. The question is made inadequately, because species do not actually develop, but only specific groups of living beings form within species do, with the rest remaining as they were before, the old species. Living beings live life for a limited time, which is the case with entire species, living life for a limited time, even if their niche is still around. Even niches are around only temporarily, as part of the comprehensive development of life.

Furthermore, the physical bodies do not develop on their own, because life develops comprehensively, body and mind, or body and intelligence. The intelligences themselves develop, yet they always develop only as entire systems of intelligences, many times expanding outside organisms and outside entire species, while developing all life simultaneously, not only the hoofs of the antelope and the heads of the cobra snakes.

There are specific developmental intelligences performing all developmental specialized tasks, while the physical bodies are not the ones conducting the adaptation to the new environment, since bodies are only physical, not cognitive in nature, and cannot think without their intelligences. Intelligences are not exactly alive within the body as fishes are alive within fish tanks, but intelligences are the physical bodies as seen from an inner subjective perspective, while the physical bodies are the intelligences themselves as these intelligences are seen from a cognitive perspective. This still might seem tedious to understand, yet it is the same with minds and brains, because minds are the brains themselves as the brains are seen from an inner subjective cognitive perspective, while the brains are the minds themselves as the minds are seen from objective material perspectives in the outside world. You are mind, body, and soul as one, from three different perspectives, subjective or cognitive, physical or objective, and higher or highjective.

The intelligences that these physical bodies hold within do the continuous, transitory process of reshaping the physical body in order to account for the changes in their existential niche. Furthermore, when studied closely, you are capable to find one intelligence from the cognitive system of all living beings of all species responsible or specialized in one specific condition of the environment, favorable or unfavorable, one on one.

Since these outside conditions change slowly, because the outside environment is alive and it develops similarly, the inner intelligences have to respond accordingly by modifying themselves and therefore by modifying the entire organism correspondently, as far and as much as their developmental specialized tasks demand. However, this change takes place within the cognitive system, because there is where the developmental intelligences live. You must study the development of life from inner subjective cognitive perspectives first, in order to understand the entire development of life. From an inner cognitive perspective, you notice how intelligences form systems of intelligences slightly differently than they did before, according to the new requirements coming straight from the change in the environment, seen from an objective material perspective as a change in the shape of the hoof or of the head. Even your own head can change visibly throughout life according to the shape of your brain, just by undergoing a university education, for your head to remain larger throughout life, just by working in an office, or smaller, just by ending your education in sixth grade.

Because if you want to understand adaptation to environment, you first have to understand exactly how you think, how all intelligences of all cognitive systems think, while science also ignores this, so you will not find it anywhere else. I discovered and named intelligences throughout this entire book series "Human," along with the intelligent human development and the development of the entire life. Science ignores systematically everything necessary for you to gain your true, accurate background knowledge allowing you to reason independently and to gain your freedom in this world. Science does so in order for you to have to depend on your drugs and money, and implicitly on your authorities for the rest of your life, or for as long as your authorities decide to keep you around, since they tend to exterminate entire genetic lines one after another, keeping only the most docile around.

Intelligences are unique, as they maintain their uniqueness throughout life, otherwise, they cease to exist by default, since identical intelligences form together a similar intelligence. While all intelligences are specialized within cellular components, cells, organisms, families, communities, societies, and entire ecosystems, counting in zillions, with one intelligence for each inner and outside specialized task, and with specialized intelligences tending to each niche element in the outside world, counting in zillions.

With each environmental change, dreadful or benefic, it is a new specialized intelligence fortunate to have its own specialization to tend to, since it has the opportunity to exist and to be part of the cognitive system, organism, species, and Life herself, yet only if it knows well how to perform the new task related to the new change in the environment, with a zillion new specialized intelligences seeking the same, many times cooperating harmoniously towards the same goal, and with a zillion old specialized intelligences helping with their own old abilities as best as they can, as this is normal, continuous development.

With every change in the environmental conditions, there are new existential niches becoming available, while the old ones become unavailable. Each new existential niche or niche element is a new opportunity for any intelligence to specialize or re-specialize, matching it and taking over it, if they only know how to do everything. If not, then you as an intelligence have nothing left to do within the cognitive system, there is no specialization for you, you become meaningless and unfulfilled, you go idle, and Life removes you from Existence at once. Since physical bodies hold directly these inner intelligences, every time intelligences specialize successfully to new existential niches, the body holding them morphs and develops physically in order to make possible the new intelligence and its new specialization, integrating within the entire cognitive system, and therefore integrating within the entire physical body.

It is this simple at the cognitive and physical level, since physical organisms are formed of specialized cells themselves, and it is always a matter of moving these around as they form the entire body, and not of modifying these cells physically directly, because these cells as you have them currently have been around in this form for a billion years at least.

Therefore, it is never a question of how organisms and entire species morph in order to match more efficiently the new tasks within the new environment, because life is not even lived entirely at the organism and species level, but life is lived mostly at the cellular level and on subcellular levels, even at the ionic and molecular levels, as these remain unchanged throughout time.

All systems of intelligences throughout all living beings are formed of systems of intelligences that are formed of systems of intelligences all the way down to the ionic intelligences living life directly on top of the electromagnetic field. The ionic intelligences are the only ones actually alive, because everything else that they form above themselves through their continuous living harmonious interconnectivity are only families, communities, and societies of themselves, only implicitly alive, because the living ionic intelligences give them life through their own life.

All molecules that all ions form throughout cells are living communities of living ions, having only an implicit life, because all ions give them life. It is similar with all cells and all organisms, because these are only societies and civilizations of ions, as all ions interconnect while forming all cellular components of all cells, then all cells, all tissue, all organs, all bodily systems, all organisms, all families, all societies, and all ecosystems, everything formed by the living ionic intelligences living life right on top of the electromagnetic field capable to form all matrices of life for all ionic intelligences and therefore for all living ions of the electromagnetic type of life.

The same ionic form of life is in stars, rock, fire, water, ice, in the ionosphere, and in the interstellar space, yet these ions form other forms of life above themselves, while their ionic intelligences interconnect in entirely different manners to form their families, communities, societies, civilizations, and entire ecosystems, according to all environmental conditions of these other mediums, yet they always form their families, communities, societies, and civilizations above regardless of their medium, in order to reach all niches of their environment in a most harmonious, efficient, fulfilling manner, while through them, reaching the same Life, as they do from all environments of all mediums capable to hold the electromagnetic type of life.

This is the reason why subcellular components and entire cells decided to live life together while forming higher and higher forms of life, in order not to put up with the outside environment anymore, so they do not have to develop anymore, but they let these higher forms of life that they form to cope with the outside environment from then on. This is why people decide to live within communities and societies, so they do not have to put up with the outside natural environment either, so they let society deal with everything. This is why I cannot find too many accurate examples to give throughout this chapter regarding the natural environment, because you do not really live too much in the real, natural environment, since you have houses, schools, factories, office buildings, supermarkets, and cars to be in, not out in the natural environment. While if you happen to be outside for a few hours or so, then you have clothes covering you as much as needed, many times impermeable, in order to keep water and humidity out.

Therefore, in your case, it is never a matter of you adapting to the environment, but a matter of adapting the environment to your needs and meanings. You can do so because you are a third level intelligent living human being, while animals are not intelligent.

This is why I have to give examples with herbivores, carnivores, and simple cells. Yet this chapter is significant for your understanding of conditions and of your reasoning and adaptation to environments, along with your understanding of inner realities, cognitive systems, and forms of life and societies, among other important concepts.

Physical bodies hold intelligences within, while intelligences develop cognitively, morphing accordingly the physical bodies holding them in a correspondent manner. Life, intelligence, and physical bodies are always correspondent, since correspondence is a supreme characteristic or law of Life. You can never have physical bodies without intelligences, since they are the same oneness, as seen from three different perspectives or correspondences, mind, body, and soul. You cannot have unintelligent life, intelligences without physical bodies, or intelligent bodies that are not alive, because the three perspectives are one, forming life. You are not only intelligent and you are not only alive, but you are one. The entire wider world is also alive and intelligent, as it is the One. You cannot consider intelligences alone as being alive without their physical body, even when they shift themselves from one body to another for various reasons, since they always have a physical body.

When you study closely physical bodies, you cannot distinguish them from the cells that they carry at scales of nanometers and lower, because nothing is rigid and material anymore at these very small scales, everything being electric and magnetic field. This field is never constant but it fluctuates, and it is this specific intelligent, modulated, encoded fluctuation or vibration becoming a matrix capable to hold inner realities, just as computers are capable to use modulated fluctuations of electricity within chips in order to form the well-known digital matrices capable to hold entire operating system that run all computer software, including the inner worlds of your videogames. Ions and molecules are capable to form the necessary matrices of life while forming entire inner subjective worlds holding all ionic intelligences that interact, work, and tend to their specializations throughout molecules, cells, organisms, societies, entire ecosystems, and Life herself. These are the intelligences of Life making her possible from inside out.

Your brain is the physical body capable to hold the inner reality of all your intelligences forming your cognitive system, which is your mind. Your brain is the objective body holding the subjective cognitive mind, and it does so through electric, magnetic, and ionic intelligent fluctuations or vibrations taking place everywhere within neurons and within neural networks. The same happens within cells, since all specialized cells and cellular components use these field fluctuations in order to form and maintain inner worlds filled with intelligences, at all levels.

There are zillions of these inner worlds within your organism including your brain, all holding zillions of inner intelligences, which are specialized, tending to all conditions at all environmental levels: inner, cognitive, social, familial, natural, and higher. Together, the body and the intelligences that it carries form life, they are alive. Similarly, the definition of life is to have a body capable to hold its own system of intelligences, within its own inner realities. Similarly, you can never have intelligences if they are not held and maintained within physical bodies, since intelligences are subjective and not objective. Therefore, they cannot exist within the physical world directly, but they exist only as they are held by physical bodies within inner realities, since the continuums of these inner realities may provide these intelligences with inner bodies. The continuum of our world is the spacetime continuum, and it manages to provide all the necessary objective bodies in this world.

This is the case throughout all realities, inner and outside, since existence within all realities is objective in nature as seen from within, while existence is seen as subjective in nature as the inner realities are seen from above. Furthermore, existence is highjective in nature higher above within upper realities, as it is seen from below and as it is seen from this world. This is why all intelligences are subjective and cognitive, because intelligences inhabit lower or inner realities, and therefore they are always subjective as seen from a higher perspective. Yet if you switch your perspective within their inner realities, you find all intelligences objective and material, as living beings, having an objective body provided to them by their own continuum, having a life, and having adjacent inner intelligences kept within additional inner realities held by those objective bodies. Similarly, from the upper perspective of our upper reality, you are seen by all souls as subjective, cognitive in nature, a simple subjective intelligence, as you work throughout life on your own specialization, and as you participate continuously throughout what it is seen from above as simple mental models and mental simulations, while you may always claim that none of what happens around you is a simulation, but it is real. Because from your own perspective, everything is objective, material, and therefore real within your own reality, and this is the case with all realities, higher and lower, when you are within them.

All intelligences are just as conscious within their own inner worlds as you are here in the outside world, since they reason similarly as you do, through all inner worlds of their own cognitive systems, since they have a cognition similar to yours. Their cognition is part of your own cognition.

As conscious intelligences, all intelligences are in charge with the interaction of their own physical body throughout their own outside world within the organism and within their own cognitive system, as it is the case with you here in the outside world. Therefore, this world is not different than any world out there or in here, while all worlds and realities of the wider world are correspondent, all having a cognitive nature.

Our own world is made possible by a common mind linking the minds of all souls coming here in this world, while it is the same with their own higher world, since all souls have souls throughout this entire cluster of created realities. It is the same with the zillions of intelligences and living beings throughout the wider world at higher and lower levels, none being different or more privileged than others, since they live, reason, and interact with their world throughout their life in very similar manners, having to cope with very similar conditions. All worlds are correspondent within inner replicas of their outside world from upper levels of reality to lower levels, replicating in this manner entire environments, one condition after another. As above so below, and as below so above, all conditions match, and therefore all meanings from the entire wider world in all its realities correspond accordingly, always being part of the meanings of Life, and therefore always being fulfilling. Yet if you take drugs and if you serve tyrants instead, your meanings diverge from the meanings of Life, ending up against Life altogether at times, and Life takes you out through your own intelligences, because your intelligences are the intelligences of Life.

Therefore, from the upper perspectives of your senses of

perception in this world, you are not the physical body, but you are an intelligence, and you refer to yourself as the conscious intelligence. You are a primal intelligence, just as your eating, recovery, and reproduction primal intelligences. Primal intelligences, just as all intelligences, are formed by smaller inner intelligences, as these interconnect continuously to help them reason through their own specialized abilities, since all intelligences are capable to form their own inner realities holding smaller intelligences within, who form inner inner realities with inner inner intelligences within, all the way down to the ionic intelligences of the ionic form of life sitting right on top of the electromagnetic field.

This is how you have realities within realities within realities, as far down as your reasoning demands. If you have to perform only a simple first level logical algorithm, then one intelligence can do this thinking immediately, because algorithmic thinking is every easy for your intelligences. Yet if you have to perform a more elaborate planning or mental model, in order to find a more complex solution, then you need an entire inner reality capable to perform the entire simulation within, and this requires additional inner realities to think through all details, additional inner inner realities opened and held by your inner intelligences participating in the mental model, down to the last necessary element of cognition, several inner realities below.

Therefore, development and adaptation to the environment are never a trial and die procedure happening in this world, with extinction taking out all unfit species as science claims, but adaptation is an entire development, where zillions of specialized intelligences simulate continuously everything happening in the outside world throughout elaborate mental models, in order to find ways to fill in all new existential niches made available by the change in all conditions of the environment, and therefore in order to determine the entire body and even the entire species to shift, form, morph, adapt, and therefore develop, by changing specific systems of intelligences to newer, better systems of intelligences.

All living beings and all intelligences develop in this manner. This is an intrinsic cognitive process of developmental mental modeling, and therefore it is never a matter of a continuous 'survive or die' trivial theory. This happens first within the cognitive system repeatedly, and if it is successful in the cognitive system, it is implemented in the outside world, mostly with the next generation, by developing directly into the new changed form. They do everything in their common mind of many living beings of the same species first, until their developmental intelligences are capable to find the successful solutions to match the change in the environment. These changes become permanent within the entire species by recording everything in the DNA of all cells of all living beings of that species, and may lead to visible morphing of the physical body in order to match perfectly and fill in that permanently different niche.

The entire developmental process is recorded in the DNA sequence, for further generations to be born directly in that changed manner. You might see it only as a change from hair horns or from small hoofs to larger hoofs, yet if you study everything closely, you notice how the entire change covers the entire organism, by also elongating the head while taking the eyes further apart, and while lengthening the neck altogether with two additional vertebras.

All these changes are recorded in the DNA, while the enzymes of all living beings of the entire species make these changes in the DNA of all cells of all organisms, or they do so only for a specific larger group within the species, leaving the rest of the species unchanged, if they are too far away, or if their own environment did not change. However, if the messenger proteins carrying the genetic change reaches them, it is more likely that their enzymes also modifies the DNA of their cells similarly, participating in the development of the entire species.

This entire comprehensive development also happens to humans, only that humans are diagnosed with cancer every time comprehensive permanent changes are made in the human DNA. The entire cellular nucleus enlarges substantially in order to make the entire developmental genetic change possible, this is diagnosed as cancer immediately, and everybody who tries to develop in any physical, cognitive, or interconnective manner is killed with nuclear radiation in less than two years. It does not matter if you are from the Masses or Brotherhood, because you are always diagnosed with cancer whenever you try to develop, regardless of how faithful you are to the entire masonry.

Therefore, not exactly species develop, but the living beings within species de. They develop now to another species, as they developed before in the past from the previous species to the current one. The living beings develop, not the species themselves. While within the living beings, the developmental intelligences develop all living beings simultaneously, through all the necessary developmental changes made directly in the DNA.

The DNA is not exactly a blueprint as science claims, but the DNA sequence is only a record of how to gather the cells that compose the organism in the exact shape and form that the parents and the entire species currently has. In order to do so, entire specialized prototype intelligences are stored in the RNA and DNA, alive, one after another, in order to be used throughout life, throughout generations, species, kingdoms, forms of life, and throughout Life herself.

The DNA is not a blueprint of life, because this is impossible in life, but the RNA and DNA are living communities of prototype intelligences, containing all the necessary specialized intelligences capable to do everything within cells, organisms, and in the outside world, or at least everything that life is capable to do, under all circumstances, including how to develop the entire life from the dawn of life to human beings in only nine months of human gestation.

For any living being, of any species, throughout gestation, the embryo and the fetus develop by following the entire DNA from the beginning to the end of that species, in order to end up looking as the parents and as the entire species do. If you study the fetus closely throughout its gestation, you find it resembling, reenacting, and reconstructing the entire development that its species has undergone throughout ages since protozoa and long before, if that species happened to have passed through the protozoa.

Because as stated, not the species develop from one to another as the current science states ignorantly, but the living beings themselves do, from one species to another ever since the dawn of the organic form of life and long before, ever since the dawn of the ionic form of life, which is the dawn of the electromagnetic type of life here on Earth. Because life is lived by the ionic intelligences, with all the molecules, cells, organisms, societies, civilizations, ecosystems, and realities that they always form, only their own interconnectivities, however they manage to interconnect wile reaching all niches of life throughout the ages of Earth, in the most efficient harmonious manner.

It might seem that the ionic intelligences can maintain a continuous similar harmony in all types, forms, and classes of life, throughout all environments in all their possible favorable and unfavorable conditions, but it is not possible, for various reasons. The ionic intelligences, and therefore the ionic living beings can reach only a limited forms and types of very stable harmonious interconnectivity, and this is how they interconnect, only in these nine distinct stable harmonious manners, which are the common nine eigen states of stable harmonious interconnectivity of life.

Only the third eigen state of stable harmonious interconnectivity is associated to humans, which is the third level intelligent stable harmonious interconnectivity, similar to what you have in the family during the good times. This was supposed to be the case everywhere in the world, as an entire comprehensive stable intelligent harmonious human family spanning the world, which is the third level living intelligent stable harmonious human society spanning the world, part of the entire third level intelligent harmonious human environment spanning the world, which is erased currently systematically in a consensual manner, while instating in its place the first level tyrannical enslaved consensual society part of the Consensual Matrix spanning most of the wider world. The human organism, the human mind, the developmental human intelligences, and humanity altogether work hard to regain the third level stable intelligent harmonious interconnectivity, always unsuccessfully, because drugs, tyrants, servitude, indoctrination, ignorance, and lack of development instate instead an artificial dogmatic bureaucratic consensual society, meant for corporations and for an entire politics and bureaucracy spanning this world, but not for living human beings. You are not even accepted in the jurisdictions of the current consensual society as a living human being, but only as a corporation.

Throughout gestation, the fetus develops in the exact manner that its entire species had undergone right until its conception. Therefore, the fetus does not exactly develop, but it actually advances, from the single cellular organism that its species had been ages ago, until the shape that the species has currently, all in the nine months of gestation.

Species never evolve, since it is impossible, because species are only societies of living beings and cannot eat on their own while they cannot reproduce on their own, but all living beings of the species eat individually, digest individually, reproduce individually, and develop individually yet similarly, within one lifetime, mostly during gestation, and they reproduce and develop in this manner since the dawn of life, but only in one lifetime, from the molecular form of life to the cellular form of life and then throughout the organic form of life throughout all species of that specific genetic line one after another, all the way to that specific generation, mostly within gestation.

It happens in this tedious manner because this is the only way that the developmental intelligences know how to connect all the necessary systems of intelligences forming all living beings exactly as it happened throughout the actual development of life from ions to humans. All developmental intelligences know well how to form all the necessary systems of intelligences from ions to living beings because they had been there themselves when it happened for billions of years ever since the dawn of life. This is how they managed to developed then throughout all environmental changes of Earth for billions of years, and therefore this is how they develop now during one lifetime, during gestation and shortly later on.

This seems true or not, because the current science never states this, while stating only random errors in the development of life while calling it evolution. Yet science never considers intelligences, including developmental intelligences.

Do all species actually develop, eat, and reproduce in this very difficult manner, while mimicking the entire development of life ever since the dawn of life in the few days, weeks, or months of gestation? Gestation is longer for advanced species, and shorter for primitive ones. Similarly, all living beings digest their food all the way dawn to the ionic form of life, with ions and amino acids included. Digestion is death through disassembly, addressing all ions and amino acids of the ionic form of life; not their own death, but only the disassembly of their own interconnectivities that took place throughout the other organisms, while using all ions and amino acids from food in the organism that ate the food, in interconnectivities specific only to the organism that ate the food.

All living beings develop very fast from molecules and cells through all their previous species, and many times they are born altogether as their previous species, to develop into their own species shortly after, throughout childhood. Yes, some living being are actually born as their previous species, and live life throughout childhood as another species altogether, as the previous species, always acting normally, as thought it is very adequate and very natural to be born as a previous species. Because species are not exactly formed of living beings, but living beings pass through all their previous species, as though they are of all species, not only of the last species. This could be true only if life is actually lived by the small ions and ionic intelligences sitting right on top of the electromagnetic field, since the electromagnetic field makes possible all their matrices of life, making all ions living beings, but only all ions, while all molecules, cells, organisms, societies, civilizations, and ecosystems above them are only their own societies and civilizations, having an implicit life through the live of all ions and ionic intelligences interconnecting into them.

Are there actually living beings born as previous species? Yes. Within the egg, all living beings are all their previous forms of life and species, including all molecules, cells, and previous species that they once were throughout the development of life, because it takes days, weeks, and months for all ions to form once again all systems of intelligences that they once were throughout the development of life ever since the dawn of life. Amphibians with frogs included, are born as fishes, while all insects are born as worms. While if you study the chicken fetus within gestating eggs, you may find there genuine, living flying reptiles. You may find the pictures and videos of the gestating chicken egg over the Internet.

Why the tedious living, intelligent endeavor to bring to life zillions of living beings since the dawn of life? Because as stated previously, you are not an individual living being, but you are a composite of trillions of cells, which are composites of just as many cellular components, now living together as an entire civilization and not as an individual living being. Because if you were an individual living being, you could have been replicated by blueprints, in an easier manner. While as an entire, complex living civilization, formed of zillions of unique living beings and intelligences, you have to reconstruct these from the beginning of their interconnectivity in this specific shape, as it takes an entire evolutionary development to do so, taking place during the first stages of life, during gestation and childhood.

Both from cognitive and physical perspectives, you are a cognitive and physical civilization, made of zillions of intelligences and living being, forming as one your objective extraordinary civilization which is the human organism. From you to the entire human civilization is only one small step, made possible by your social developmental intelligences through all your social, developmental, and civilized needs that they send you continuously. All ionic intelligences making everything possible from within you are immortal, along with all their interconnectivities that they form above, which are their families, societies, and civilizations. In order to reproduce entire organisms, you cannot simply replicate their multitude of intelligences, since it is impossible, because these are unique, but you have to carry them wholly from one generation to another as entire colonies or samples of civilizations at the moment of conception, allowing them to develop throughout gestation to reach the form and shape of the previous generation of your current species.

These are the same intelligences, alive now in you, ever since the dawn of life. As you study them closely, you find them pertinent in everything specialized that they do throughout the mind, body, family, and society, because they have been doing everything in this manner since the dawn of life, for billions of years throughout all Earth ages, very successfully, or you were not here to tell the story. The cortex itself was developed a few million years ago throughout the first golden human ages that allowed intelligent human interconnectivity both within the human mind and in the outside world in the intelligent human society, otherwise the human cortex was not here currently to confirm it. All developmental intelligences from the human cortex send you intelligent human needs continuously to develop at the intelligent human level, and this is why you read these books. The same developmental human intelligences send you needs to interconnect with everybody else in an intelligent harmonious manner throughout win-win interconnectivities, exactly as you do at home in the family, but in the entire world. The current consensual society works hard to stop you from interconnecting harmoniously intelligently within the human cognition and in the outside world in the intelligent human society, while in this manner, you erase continuously the third level intelligent human environment, keeping it replaced with the current first level consensual politics and bureaucracy making all drugs, all dogma, all tyrants, and all servants possible.

Now we can integrate this entire topic to the human condition, because all your intelligence are specialized with all environmental conditions, favorable and unfavorable, from your inner, outside, social, and higher environment. This is how all specialized intelligences are possible, in a one to one interconnectivity between all specialized intelligences of your cognitive system and all environmental conditions addressing you, counting in zillions, while the entire environment is alive in itself, consisting in similar inner intelligences forming all its conditions. All harmony is possible through win-win interconnectivities between you and all your environments. Throughout development and throughout your subsistence, by storing within your nucleic acid all your successful specialized prototype intelligences, you store implicitly all conditions of your environment, formed of similar intelligences. You do not store these directly as you do with your own specialized prototype intelligences, but you store only their replicas, their knowledge, tendencies, and behavior found within your own specialized intelligences, since these are the solutions to all environmental conditions themselves. These are your successful inner specialized intelligences standing behind all outside condition, while making subsistence and development possible. You have to do so to be able to fulfill your needs within this environment throughout life, throughout subsistence, and then throughout the rest of your genetic line, as you remember how to do everything through your prototype specialized intelligences from your DNA, counting in zillions, since they are the ones who know how to cope with each condition of all your environments, as your subconscious, conscious, classconscious, highconscious, familial, consensual, social, artistic, spiritual, and natural.

Why doing everything? Because everything that you do in life you do to fulfill your needs and meanings, while these should always be part of the meanings of life. You develop throughout gestation and throughout childhood to resemble your parents in everything that they look, are, know, and do, and more, because you have everything in you, you have all these inner intelligences specialized in everything that was necessary for your subsistence throughout your entire genetic line, ever since protozoa and long before. Since all your intelligences are specialized in all environmental conditions, of all your environments, you do not develop only yourself, only the human organism, but you develop the entire human environment just as well, with the human family, the human society, the human civilization, the intelligent human environment, and the entire human ecosystem included, since this is how higher forms of life and higher classes of life are formed.

Through your developmental primal intelligences, you do not develop only your organism, but your entire society, civilization, community, family, social structure, and entire ecosystem of Earth, alongside all the other human beings and living beings of Earth, because they have similar cognitive, developmental, social, and interconnective needs coming from all their developmental intelligences counting in zillions, while they never work one against another, but only harmoniously, at the second intuitive harmonious level, and at the third intelligent harmonious level.

This means that life itself never develops randomly or accidentally as the current science states, but it always develops in an intuitive and intelligent manner. Similarly, you never develop the human society and the human civilization in any manner possible, but you develop the entire organism, the entire human society, and the entire civilization exactly as these were throughout the previous ages, species, kingdoms, and forms of life, in the best manner that was the case then according to the current environment as it is now and considerably improved, since you have everything harmonious, intuitive, and intelligent in you, and you can always make it possible in the entire world. However, if you take drugs, you disregard the needs and meanings of all your developmental intelligences, confusing continuously your boredom and loneliness with zero level addicted needs for drugs, tyranny, and entertainment. Boredom and loneliness are not needs, but they are inner punishments for failing your developmental and interconnective needs. You do not have to entertain and to medicate your children whenever they are bored, lonely, and restless, but you can help them learn, train, and interconnect intelligently and harmoniously with everybody else.

This is the case throughout a normal, natural, intelligent human development and natural intelligent human condition, because within consensual worlds and societies as the current ones, you develop and interact in a forced manner, to form the kind of worlds and societies that you now have. You do so on behalf of an entire Consensual Matrix, which knows well this entire knowledge, as it uses it on its own behalf, against you, against your human nature, and against everything that you are and that you can become. Otherwise, it cannot subdue and exploit you as it always does, since only in this manner, it can make all drugs, all dogma, all tyrants, and all slaves possible, which are the worst human condition, so dreadful, that they make entire dark ages possible, and they never end.

Not only that the Consensual Matrix ruins you human nature, meaning, and fulfillment in Life and in this world for its own consensual existence, but by constraining you to live your life within deliberately enforced environments, your intelligences develop crookedly and inadequately, this is what they store in your nucleic acid, tyranny and servitude, this is how your prototype specialized intelligences become, tyrants and slaves, and this is the kind of worlds that they will ever develop throughout your future genetic line for ages, species, and entire worlds to come, the Consensual Matrix, meant for slavery, indoctrination, and exploitation, since this is why the dark ages never end.

This is why Life destroys and discards all meaningless, unfulfilling, improper, inadequate living beings, genetic lines, nations, species, societies, civilizations, and entire ecosystems, words, and realities of these, because once your own developmental intelligences start developing crookedly, away from the meanings and fulfillment of Life, they can never recover, and they are discarded, along with all living beings, species, and entire worlds and realities of these. Once you take your first drugs and once you start following tyrants and dogma, do not expect to recover and to become fulfilling for Life and for the world anymore, since it is too late, because you will always lack the necessary intelligent development to fulfill Life and the real world. Only the Consensual Matrix keeps you alive from then on, to serve it, apart from the meanings and fulfillment of life, while you make all drugs, dogma, and tyrants possible, necessary to contort everybody else, including your children and loved ones, and including the children and loved ones of everybody else. This is the worst human condition of all, making all dark ages possible, while these never end, until our Creator and Life herself end them.

This is the actual human condition at all levels, always contorted and always dreadful, and this is what it does in Life and in the wider world. If you serve in a hierarchic brotherhood, at any social level, you know exactly what your entire servitude is meant to do in Life, in the Consensual Matrix, and in the real world, because the Consensual Matrix owns all hierarchic brotherhoods and uses them systematically to alter the human nature, meaning, fulfillment, genome, and entire future, on its own consensual behalf. This had been the case ever since the Sumerians and long before, contorting humanity altogether to the point where it cannot subsist and develop anymore on its own, apart from the Consensual Matrix, lacking the necessary knowledge and abilities to fulfill Life. Humanity cannot survive without the Consensual Matrix anymore, with Life herself discarding it once the Consensual Matrix pulls away.

Individual organisms have the choice to live life independently, or they may gather within classes of life in order to live life there, through various advantages and disadvantages. This is how molecules gather to form cells, cells gather to form organisms, and humans gather to form the multitude of hierarchies, ideologies, and jurisdictions spanning society, as all current consensual hierarchic brotherhoods. Humanity was supposed to form the intelligent harmonious human society, yet it forms all consensual jurisdictions, hierarchies, and ideologies instead, with the current consensual masonry in the West, and with the current consensual radical political ideologies and radical religious ideologies in the East, marking the most dreadful human conditions both in the West and in the East, while in this manner, integrating humanity in the Consensual Matrix entirely, as the Consensual Matrix spans most of the wider world, where everything is a similar dark age, since this is how it came here, and this is how it goes everywhere else. Nothing in the Consensual Matrix is part of Life and of the meanings of Life, by law and by ideology, since they do not even allow you in the jurisdictions of the Consensual Matrix as a living human being, but only as a consensual corporation, always doing as told.

Forms of life are built one on top of another, with the ionic form of life at the base of the molecular form of life, at the base of the cellular form of life, at the base of the organic form of life. All intelligences have their roots in the electromagnetic field. By interconnecting in systems of intelligences and in systems of systems of intelligences, all your intelligences transcend from one form of life to another to reach and to be able to coordinate entire organisms throughout all their primal specializations, as eating, recovery, development, reproduction, learning, social, and security.

Furthermore, since life is not lived individually, but in entire lifelines of existence, as in the mind body soul simple model, you still find these same intelligences throughout your entire lifeline of existence and in all its spheres of interconnectivity. The human condition expands many times to cover your entire lifeline of existence, even though the human condition should remain restraint to the last sphere, the social sphere of interconnectivity, or social sphere of influence, with the entire interconnectivity taking place in this sphere, conducted by and through the human condition.

This is your social human sphere of interconnectivity. If

you lived your life isolated from society, in nature throughout pristine environments, you had your natural human conditions, defining your human sphere of interconnectivity, all made possible by your outside self, the physical body, or the organism, as this interacts in this world throughout the fulfillment of all its needs.

Therefore, for the organic form of life, cells are of the first class, organisms of the second, families and genetic lines of the third, species of the fourth, societies of the fifth, civilizations of the sixth, realities of the seventh, clusters of realities of the eighth, up to Life herself. These are alive, only that they are of different forms or classes, with life present at all levels of forms of life and classes of life. Throughout your life, you have to remain aware of all forms of life and classes of life that you form and that compose you, since you have to tend to them throughout life, because they send you needs through all their intelligences from all their levels. They hold intelligences at all levels, and these send you their needs, or they send you only the needs that they cannot fulfill themselves.

Why do all these primal, specialized intelligences send you their needs? Why can't they fulfill their needs themselves? Because you as a conscious intelligence are responsible with the activity of the entire organism in the outside world, while your subconscious intelligences are specialized in everything within the organism, as recover, circulation, and digestion. Your developmental intelligences address cells, organisms, families, societies, and entire ecosystems, yet these only send you their developmental needs as they want, while you as a conscious intelligence must fulfill them in the outside world, along with all social, security, and physiological needs coming from your subconscious intelligences.

Everything that you do in life you do in order to fulfill your needs and meanings at the level of all your cells, intelligences, those around, their intelligences, and all interconnectivities that you form with all those around and with their intelligences. You do so on behalf of your cells, you feed them and you recover them, you breathe for them and you give them food, water, shelter, and security, while you do the same for your family, society, humanity, and the entire ecosystem of Earth, while also developing them in all details, if you are ever allowed. You make sure that you reproduce, as much as you are allowed, in order to keep these higher classes of life alive after you die. You also learn and develop yourself in order to cope with society and to fit in society, you specialize just as well in order to work within society, and you train and teach the young ones to specialize, passing to them your entire knowledge and experience. You do all these through needs and meanings, normal and consensual, and you are always rewarded when you are successful, or you are punished if you neglect anything or if you are unsuccessful.

If you remain unaware of all these, you will never be able to identify your higher needs of higher classes, and you suffer accordingly, because you are always punished by your intelligences every time you fail fulfilling them. This is why you have to take drugs throughout life, in order to cancel the pain, or only to feel meaningful and fulfilled in life, as you attempt to do at the zero addicted level through drugs, making everything dreadful. Drugs are always the worst human condition, because they never make you feel good, but dreadfully, ruining your entire living human meaning and living human fulfillment.

This is why you are diagnosed with bipolar disorder, because sometimes you fulfill your higher needs and sometimes you do not, and this is how you are punished sometimes and rewarded the rest. You feel up and down for no reason, so you assume that you must be sick, because you do not feel good continuously throughout life as you always expect. Yet you never associate your feelings with the entire punishment-reward mechanism that your intelligences use in order to determine you to fulfill their needs throughout life, since you are the conscious intelligence specialized with the entire interaction of the organism in the outside world.

You are responsible with the new activities of the organism throughout the outside world as you use it in order to fulfill all needs sent to you by all your intelligences. These intelligences are capable to fulfill their own needs, only that, when the environment changes, they become incapable to do so, and they make you fulfill everything, for them. They make you work hard to find a solution to do the job for them, for as long as the environmental conditions remain new for them. Because when they master all environmental conditions, they can do everything even on their own.

For example, if you were always able to get your water from the faucet in order to drink and wash yourself, now without water coming from your faucet for various reasons, you have to find another source of water, or you have to repair the old one. If you manage to repair it, you fulfill successfully your need in the outside world, and your intelligences do not bother you anymore, because they already know where the water is and how to use it on their behalf. Yet if you have to find other sources of water or if you have to modify the old one, then the entire routine changes, the old intelligences are incapable to occupy their old existential niche, and new intelligences have to take over the new routine, getting water from the bathroom faucet instead, to wash the dishes. It takes you a few days of getting used to the other type of faucet, which you have just bought and installed. You always have to use your conscious mind at first, while you get used to the new faucet, yet by the next week, you will be using the new faucet without even paying conscious attention to what you are doing, because it is not exactly you doing the dishes when you are used to do everything in all details, but it is one of the multitude of your subconscious intelligences, as it works flawlessly throughout its new faucet specialization. You notice the direct relationship between your own specialized intelligences and all environmental conditions, old and new.

As a conscious intelligence, you are responsible only with the new interactions of your organism in the outside world, as you tend to all new conditions, continuously throughout life. This is the life condition of your conscious intelligence, which is an inner self of yours, and not of the entire organism, which is your outside self or physical body. Conditions change continuously, and you always have to find a way to deal with them, and therefore you must always find successful solutions to cope with the environment. How do you do everything?

Let us see first how your subconscious intelligences manage your old conditions, through all your old routines. This is a very simple procedure, since it involves only a casual stimulus – response procedure, as problem – solution, or need – fulfillment, which all your subconscious intelligences can do well. However, with every change in the niche, environment, or conditions, this simple procedure is no longer viable, since your subconscious intelligences cannot perform them anymore, because they do not have access to your entire interaction of the organism in the outside world, but only to that specific routine. Because you as a conscious intelligence are responsible with the entire interaction of the organism in the outside world, and therefore now it is your job to solve the problem.

This is how the newly specialized intelligences become alive within developing species to make them capable to cope, subsist, and develop while never becoming extinct, just as you as a conscious intelligence are capable to cope on your own with all changes of your immediate environment, while always helped and constrained by all your conscious, subconscious, and inner intelligences throughout life, throughout society, throughout this world, and throughout your fulfillment. Species do not evolve, since it is impossible to do so, as it is even ignorant to assume so, but the living beings and the intelligences themselves develop continuously, throughout continuously changing environmental conditions.

While your intelligences were capable to keep your equilibrium as you rode your bike, now with the sudden flat tire, they cannot do so anymore, and you either find a conscious solution fast to stabilize yourself on the bike, you do so by involving your conscious reasoning at your best, or if not, you fall off your bike and you are injured, with all your intelligences punishing you strongly through all pain and regret that you will ever feel. Your intelligences will never forgive you when you fail, since you tend to compromise them continuously anyway. In an undeveloped consensual world, all intelligences already know that the conscious intelligence itself is a dreadful condition for the entire cognitive system, compromising everyone and everything, the entire cognition, and therefore the entire society. You are always their condition, dreadful or not, your choice.

You are constrained through consensual social conditions to act and to behave against your own cognitive system and entire organism, or against your family and all your loved ones, but mostly against other people or against the entire world. This is the most dreadful human condition currently and throughout history, having people against people in this world, even in organized groups and societies. Imagine that your parents fight continuously at home, since this is how people interact one against another continuously throughout the current consensual society, just by using money or just by using hierarchies, ideologies, authorities, and jurisdictions.

In order for you to have more money, others must have less, because money is constant in this world. Money itself places you against others, to the point where you actually end up killing the very poor and the very vulnerable throughout the poor nations, because the money that you have, you take from them. You always have people against people in an undeveloped consensual world, in very large numbers. Ideologies and jurisdictions unite people against people in very large numbers, to help them gain wealth and social power in an organized manner, taking form the poor and from the vulnerable of this world.

You might assume that this entire financial, ideological, and juridical discrimination, exploitation, and extermination has to end eventually, whenever these few miserable very poor people of this world die, but it never ends, since there are always bottom social layers in this world after the old bottom social layers die away, soon to be your turn, alongside your loved ones, since you tend to share the same social layer.

This happens currently with the Masses and the Lower

Brotherhood, until the entire Brotherhood goes extinct. With the nonvisible kingdom, Brotherhood, and the Elite following soon, since nobody comes to save you from yourselves, but you will always serve and you will always be tyrants, in any consensual manner that you choose.

With you always willing to harm others, because it is legal and it is very common, as it is always the case throughout business transactions, throughout wars, or throughout organized crime. This should never surprise you in an undeveloped consensual world, while you should never ask for help to save you from yourselves whenever your time comes.

How do you cope with all new problems throughout the outside world? Through intelligent reasoning, because you have a cortex, otherwise you have to do everything intuitively from your midbrain, or reflexively from the basal ganglia, yet it is less successful. Everything that you do in life you do in order to fulfill your needs, yet you always have to fulfill only needs related to new conditions and new environmental changes, because your subconscious intelligences take care of the rest of your needs, of your old needs, through old routines and old procedures.

How do you take care of your new needs? You do so through reasoning. Furthermore, you always reason throughout life only in order to cope with new circumstances while you fulfill your needs. If you are tempted to argue that you always reason throughout life under all circumstances and not necessarily related to needs, just monitor yourself throughout the day or throughout the week to see how everything that you do and think relates to your needs, as security, social, eating, reproductive, entertainment, drugs, development, and learning. These are needs of all levels, and you fulfill them either intelligently through reasoning, intuitively through feelings and thinking combined, or consensually through all your legal and ideological connections in the current consensual hierarchic society.

Drugs and entertainment are your needs of the zero level, which are your needs for pleasure itself. These are unnecessary and harmful, and you end up suffering throughout life when you fulfill them. Yet they have a natural purpose at their core, since the need for pure pleasure constrains you to fulfill all your needs in the first place, since if you never enjoy the rewards of pleasure that your intelligences give you, if you never crave for this highly pleasant feeling throughout life, you would not become engaged in any of your activities, your tasks would remain unfulfilled and even unidentified, and you die while wondering what goes on.

It is in this specific need for pure pleasure that you tap every time you take your drugs, and by doing so, you end up interfering with the entire punishment-reward mechanism. Since pleasure is constant, and it always burns your receptors when you receive too much or when you enforce it for too long, and therefore you will stop receiving it for your basic fulfillment, taking you away from the meanings and fulfillment of Life. You will never engage in your basic fulfillment of needs, your needs remain unfulfilled, and your life goes down from there. All you will seek from then on is pure pleasure and nothing else. With you not fulfilling your needs, you do not count for Life anymore, you do not count for society anymore, you do not count for your family anymore, and all these dispose of you in every manner. This is the zero, addicted human condition, always unfavorable, the worst that you can have. Yet all souls come here for drugs, in order to be and become the worst, compromising this entire world by default.

It is you the conscious intelligence many times training or instating the new intelligences tending to the new environmental conditions, while your other primal subconscious intelligences do the same, throughout their own specializations. If the new environmental conditions remain instated for centuries or millennia, and if they are significant throughout life, then these new specialized intelligences develop themselves accordingly within the organism, many times altering or reshaping the entire organism to enhance their fulfillment and therefore their success. This is how entire species develop larger hoofs and longer horns, or other times, they recycle old features and specializations according to all environmental conditions, and this is how scales become feathers or hair, with the same specialized intelligences tending to them. This is how cellular membranes become skin and then they become brains, with you caught in all these physical structures continuously as a conscious intelligence. After billions of years of continuous specialized conscious work throughout various forms of life, kingdoms, species, and races, you even have the chance to read about these in a book.

How exactly do you reason while you fulfill all your needs related to the new conditions and related to the new changes in the environment? You find a solution. You always find a solution, through trial and errors called mental models. Otherwise, without thinking first, you must do everything directly in the outside world, unsuccessfully, as when you have to park your car in a tight spot. You may try and try in this world until you get it right, or you may reason instead, performing the entire maneuver in your mind first, as a mental model, or as a mental simulation of the outside circumstance, until you find the best scenario, the best solutions, the best maneuver to park your car, mostly in a better parking spot nearby. Once you find your solution, you apply it in real life, it is successful just as it was in your mind, and you avoid damaging doors and fenders in the process. Because you have already damaged all cars around including yours throughout your mental models, but you did so in your mind, throughout your reasoning, which is harmless in the outside world. You learned from your experience, and you do not want to repeat it both in your mind and in the outside world.

All intelligences mental model throughout all specialized tasks within the organism and in the outside world, thinking in mental models first, before they perform their newer, more tedious specialized tasks within the organism. While asking for help if their tasks relate to other specializations, by sending needs and feelings to all relevant surrounding specialized intelligences, including you the conscious intelligence, to do your part in the outside world.

There is more taking place in this world besides a continuous dreadful extinction, since living beings and intelligences act against death and against extinction continuously, throughout entire mental models involving all living beings and intelligences. If this world is an entire cognitive mental model, caught in the entire Universal Mind of the wider world throughout Life, always carrying its own developmental meaning in Life and in the wider world, then life and this world are significantly more complex, more meaningful, and more fulfilling than the trivial explanation given by science that the incapable goes extinct while the capable gets to live, and this is how life develops and copes with the environment. The wider world is not even the environment of Life, but everything is alive in the wider world, with Life and Intelligence always making the wider world possible, one reality after another from the inside out.

Is the parking lot itself alive, allowing you to cope with the tight parking space for half an hour while frying your brains? What exactly is alive in this entire unfortunate experience? Your successful idea to park somewhere else, otherwise, you spend half an hour to park your car while becoming frustrating. While parking the car, you have used the same conscious inner intelligences to park your car in your mind, as you use them in the real world to park your actual car. You can even see them on the display of an EEG machine as they perform this specific maneuver in your mind and in this world while lighting up similarly. They might not even distinguish your mental models from the real world, rewarding you in both instances similarly for your driving success. These inner intelligences remain linked to their specific environmental conditions continuously, since this is their task, and this is what they always do. It is the same with all your inner intelligences, counting in zillions. This is a supreme characteristic of Life, called Mentalism, which is also a natural law of the universe.

How do you perform these mental models? You do so just as your own intelligences do their routines, through stimulus – response procedures. Only that, since you act in the outside world, now you need all the relevant data of the outside world throughout the mental model, and this means that you must have it stored in your conscious inner mind world first, as previous knowledge. Once you have all the necessary knowledge, you place it together in a larger system of intelligences, which is the actual mental model or intelligent conception, which is the actual plan or procedure. You try it in your mind first, and if it works, you use it to apply everything in the outside world.

Yet your mental model, system of knowledge, plan, procedure, or intelligent conception do not work in your mind from the first trial, and you must redo everything in your mind, the entire mental model, plan, procedure, or intelligent conception, until it works, which might be frustrating. This is how you park the car, repair the faucet, save your marriage, and learn everything about human conditions, always in your mind first, through similar mental models, continuous elaboration, dozens of mental trials, and additional plans and procedures, until you conceive the entire intelligent conception as an actual system of intelligences formed of everything that you know in this topic, along with everything that you must invent yourself.

This is how you solve all your problems while fulfilling all your needs as a conscious intelligence in the outside world, in your mind first. This is how all your specialized subconscious intelligences fulfill all their specialized tasks within the organism, and this is how all developmental intelligences have always been successful while developing the entire life through all forms of life and classes of life, through similar tedious intuitive and or intelligent mental models, never randomly, neither carelessly, nor accidentally. Since you are mind, body, and soul, everything that developmental intelligences achieve in the mind first, it transposes correspondently in the outside world, as a developmental change of the entire organism.

Every time your developmental intelligences were successful to cope with all unfavorable environmental conditions, they became a specialized intelligence of the entire cognitive system, responsible from then on with the fulfillment of all specialized needs related to that environmental condition. This is how all your specialized conscious, subconscious, classconscious, and highconscious intelligences were conceived, many times very similarly to how you conceive right now your third level intelligent conception of the human condition while reading this book and while reasoning intelligently in parallel with this book, always at your third intelligent human level. When your third level intelligent conception of the human condition is completed, you will be able to wear it cognitively as a glove while reasoning intelligently through it, or as it, since it is the same. Additionally, all your intelligent conceptions spanning the cortex are capable to reason intelligently on their own while interconnecting continuously with the same goal, to help you throughout your intelligent reasoning, because all your intelligent conceptions are alive throughout your cortex, normal living beings within your own conscious intelligent inner mind world spanning the cortex, where you live your life as the intelligent inner self.

This is why you have to assess the circumstance even before you start your reasoning, in order to know your initial conditions well: how tight the parking spot is, how expensive the cars around are, how well you have succeeded before, and how worried your family is. You memorize these, and then you perform your mental simulation just as you would drive in the outside world.

Since you drive in the outside world mostly through your inner intelligences after twenty years of driving, you are actually using throughout your mental simulation these exact intelligences that drive and park your car in the outside world whenever conditions are old and easy, and whenever you have to think at something else or you have to talk with someone else, as you always do. It is not you driving then, but your subconscious specialized driving intelligences. You still engage your own conscious attention when the traffic becomes more demanding or too unpredictable to be followed by your subconscious intelligences, and you take control consciously then. These subconscious driving intelligences do your real driving throughout life when the road conditions are old and easy, while you use these same subconscious intelligences in order to perform your mental models for everything related to driving. For them, it is nothing new, since they are used to driving, because driving is their only life, and they might not even realize that they are only in a mental simulation and not in the real world. While for you it is simple reasoning, you have always thought in this manner, and you have never cared how everything takes place in your mind.

Well before your entire species is doomed to die away and go extinct as the theory of evolution predicts, by failing to cope with the environment, there are zillions of intelligences throughout zillions of living beings failing and succeeding throughout zillions of mental models, together rendering the entire humanity successful and extinct, but only in the mind. Because eventually, they find all the necessary successful solutions meant to keep everything going smoothly and even harmoniously and prosperously in the outside world, as they always do.

Not all species go extinct. You may study humans throughout gestation, to find there many species to have gone extinct throughout the ages of Earth, yet these are not exactly gone, because they are us, and we are still around. Can we still believe that some species go extinct while others manage to succeed and this is life, when the species that are not around anymore are actually the ones that are still around? Because species do not evolve as science states ignorantly, but their living beings develop throughout the ages and throughout their own life from one species to another. Species are not formed of living beings, but living beings go through all their species, from the moment of conception throughout gestation. These are only their species, everything that they had been through ever since the dawn of life, while all those species are still around, through them.

Development itself is a supreme characteristic of Life, as it always manifests in Life and in the wider world, while this is not the supreme characteristic of extinction of Life as the current consensual science depicts it, but an actual developmental supreme characteristic of Life.

How are your subconscious intelligences capable to drive your car throughout the new circumstances of your mental simulations if these are new, and therefore your subconscious intelligences should never be able to cope with them? Nothing is new entirely, but only specific components are new throughout your new conditions, as the parking spot being too small or too hard to get it because of other cars parked crooked all around. This is why you have to find a solution through your own conscious reasoning. Your intelligences already know how to park the car under many other old circumstances, since they have been doing so successfully for years. Now, you have to risk your maneuver by trying it directly, or you have to do so in your mind several times ahead, in order to see if it works. Either way, you still perform this maneuver through the same subconscious driving intelligences, while monitoring and helping them consciously, through the same cognitive procedures. Only that you do so in your mind first, faster, and with no harmful results, because you have newly encountered elements throughout the entire procedure. It is only for these specific new elements that you have to find a solution, and you may tend to them in a conscious manner by driving the car in your mental model consciously whenever the mental model reaches the tedious new stage. You do so through a trial and error procedure because you will also fail the first times even as a conscious intelligence, since everything is new to you, or you may perform your mental model directly intelligently, if you are developed at the third intelligent level.

You do everything in your mind first, through the same intelligences that do everything in the outside world, with no difference for your entire cognitive system in your mind or in the real world.

Once your mental model is successful, you park the car in the real world as you did in your mind. Then you memorize how you did everything successfully, in order to remember it the next time when you choose again to park your car in inadequate places, so you do not have to invent or discover the same solution all over again.

This is how you form your new inner conscious specialized intelligences yourself, by remembering everything that you did right and how you did everything, by conceiving everything into a larger living conception in your mind, which is the actual new living specialized intelligence responsible with this entire new parking technique.

Your knowledge is not stored in books and entire libraries of books containing all techniques needed to perform everything throughout life, and now every time you have to remember how to do everything you simply search throughout these mind books and you find out how to do everything, but throughout your intelligent conscious mind, which is your entire intelligent replica of the world, you have all concepts and conceptions of everything that you know, understand, perceive, and remember, which are your actual memories, and they are genuine intelligences themselves, and you use them directly to perform your conscious tasks, since they know exactly what they have to do. Your own inner conscious intelligences already know everything that they have to do consciously, in a living manner.

Sometimes, your inner conscious intelligences may act directly in this world, if they know well what to do, while other times, they require through needs and feelings your continuous supervision as a conscious intelligence, performing the entire procedure together. While there are times when you simply embody your inner conscious intelligences to perform the entire task yourself as them, or through them, since the cognitive interconnectivity is very diverse within the human mind.

As a reference, concepts or conceptions are alive, since you actually give birth to them in your intelligent inner replica of the world, as you do with all memories and understandings of the outside world every time you learn and elaborate them.

Your memories and understandings are your concepts and conceptions, which are also your inner conscious intelligences counting in zillions, as they are all alive and intelligent, being genuine intelligences themselves, and many times thinking and reasoning on their own. With you simply waiting for their own successful ideas to pop up in your mind, and you call this reasoning. While you were supposed to mental model intelligently alongside them continuously, as a conscious intelligence, since this is the actual human rationality.

Yet since you never learn in school how you actually reason, because the current science cannot understand the human mind, the human rationality, and the entire human cognition, along with the human meaning, human conditions, human fulfillment, human survival, human development, and the entire human life, it creates an entire undeveloped world, with you undeveloped in it continuously. With the current science also stating that you are random or accidental in life and in the world.

These specialized inner conscious intelligences are found by the zillions within your conscious system of intelligences, since every conscious ability that you have as a conscious intelligence of the entire organism is actually an inner specialized intelligence when you consider it at its own perspective, since this is how you form the entire conscious mind, which is the entire intelligent replica of the world spanning the cortex, made possible throughout your continuous lifelong learning and lifelong experience.

You train your subconscious intelligences the successful solutions, as you allow them to use them in the outside world, since you have other conscious tasks to tend to in very large numbers, and you cannot do everything on your own. This is how you reason, and this is how you live your life. Yet if your other intelligences cannot succeed in the outside world on their own, they send you needs and feelings immediately to help them, since your specialization is the entire outside world. You feel slight feelings of fear then, along with a very determined need to pay more attention while driving, and this is how you solve the entire traffic problem and how you train your intelligences furthermore. While in low traffic, you can drive for hours doing everything else as a conscious intelligence, since your other intelligences drive very well on their own.

You reason in this manner continuously throughout life, through mental simulations performed within already memorized existing circumstances of the outside world. Since you have to memorize both the existing circumstances and the successful solutions, you end up memorizing the entire successful procedure and circumstance, which is the entire event of the outside world. Yet since you have been reasoning in this manner for life, you have already memorized all circumstances, all facts, all objects, and all people, everything from the outside world that you have ever interacted with and that was tedious and important enough to draw your conscious attention and your conscious reasoning. Everything is in your mind, in form of memories, all your concepts and conceptions, ready for you to use them as needed throughout all your future mental models.

As you gather all your memories throughout your lifelong understanding, learning, perception, and experience in the outside world, you do not dump them in your intelligent conscious mind spanning the cortex randomly, you do not index them in large data basis either, but you place them in your intelligent mind exactly as they are found in the outside world, while linking them furthermore through further correlation and further understanding called elaboration. This is your intelligent mind world, which is also an intelligent inner replica of the outside world achieved in a correspondent manner with the outside world, while as a conscious intelligence, you are its creator, and this is your world, always part of the wider world.

This entire summation of memories and successful ideas is a replica of the outside world, all in your mind, populated with all people that mean anything for you in the outside world, all alive in your mind, all represented by living inner intelligences, as they live and simulate everything that you ever need throughout all your intelligent social mental models from your inner replica of the world. Yet you have replicas of everything in your intelligent conscious mind, not only replicas of people, but also of all objects and subjects of the outside world.

As a conscious intelligence, you also live your life in your intelligent inner replica of the world. However, as a conscious intelligence, you originate in the entire organism, not only in your cortex. Therefore, in order for you to live your life in your intelligent inner replica of the world, you must have a body or self there, which is your intelligent inner self. You had also created your intelligent inner self in your intelligent inner replica of the world, through everything that you perceive, know, understand, and expect yourself to be in the outside world. Your intelligent inner self from your intelligent inner replica of the world is the intelligent replica of your physical body from the outside world. As a conscious intelligence, you are there as your intelligent inner self, and this is how you live your life in the intelligent inner replica of the world spanning the cortex, as the intelligent inner self from the left prefrontal cortex, but only while mental modeling social circumstances from the outside world regarding yourself. Otherwise, you embody or impersonate other people if you must make intelligent social mental models regarding them.

Similarly, as a conscious intelligence, you can embody or impersonate all your memories, concepts, understandings, and conceptions of your intelligent conscious mind, to live your life through them or as them for as long as you must reason in those topics. While right now as you read this book, you embody or impersonate mostly your third level intelligent conception of the human condition, because this is the topic of this book. If needed, you must also embody or impersonate all related third level intelligent concepts and conceptions, depending on your topic of rationality. You can embody or impersonate the third level conceptions of intelligence, mind, cognition, reality, understanding, elaboration, intelligences, system of intelligences, society, tyranny, consensus, doctrine, meaning, Life, and the wider world.

You can embody and impersonate everything from your entire conscious mind, all your inner conscious intelligences, while you can also relocate all your memories, understandings, concepts, and conceptions in order to form new systems of intelligences as new living intelligent concepts and conceptions on any new topic that you had discovered yourself while reading these books, because they are very vast.

It is easier to form systems of intelligences by using intelligent concepts than entire conceptions, because you must disassemble conceptions first into concepts, throughout your entire understanding, reassembling these concepts into new intelligent conceptions exactly as you discover them. This is why you have a cortex, and this is why the organic form of life worked hard to develop a cortex right on top of your midbrain, to allow you to store all intelligent conceptions and conceptual elements found in the outside world, which are exactly these elemental environmental conditions in all their details as they are in the outside world. Everything is in your mind, everything is in you, and when these environmental conditions are significant and last for ages, they become part of your genetic line and entire species. Since if they are meaningful enough, these newly specialized inner intelligences have to be stored as prototypes in your DNA, in both strains simultaneously, for an increased accuracy.

Living beings are not exactly formed and born within environments, but they are the environments themselves, while the entire environment is them, since by now, their entire living condition is in all living beings, in the entire world. This is how all are one and one is all, the One.

While now we want to know how they do so. Everything is objective and material in all worlds and realities for as long as you are there. It is the same with your intelligent inner replica of the world and with all your inner mind realities, conscious and subconscious, since for all your intelligences inhabiting them, everything is objective and material. With all conditions of the outside world part of their direct, real condition within the inner replica of the world, and therefore with everything happening in your inner replica of the world correspondent to the outside world.

And now, with all your intelligences inhabiting your inner replica of the world by the zillions, and with everything correspondent, objective, and material, all events, achievements, and circumstances that your intelligences themselves undergo and experience in your inner replica of the world throughout their normal lives there, become very useful for you as a conscious intelligence, since you may expect and use them correspondently in the outside world.

Your inner conscious intelligences actually drive real cars in your mind, within your inner replica of the world, since your inner replica of the world is a genuine reality in itself, as it is even objective in nature when you are within as an intelligence. All environmental conditions are already there, as objects, subjects, understandings, concepts, and circumstances, in form of intelligences, since everything from your inner world is a living intelligence, regardless of what it represents there, a car, a person, the parking lot, or you the inner self driving the car.

As you study Life through all her living beings and intelligences from all her forms of life and realities, you find her formed of life and intelligences, at all levels, and in all details. It is the same with you, since you are part of Life, and you are alive in all your details and components, physical, cognitive, social, artistic, spiritual, and higher, including your memories, feelings, needs, and intelligences.

There are many types of inner replicas of this world. So far in our example, we had an accurate, well-elaborated replica of the world, in as many inner environmental conditions as possible, all very well understood rationally at the third intelligent human level. Yet within first level consensual inner replicas of this world, you have beliefs, stereotypes, and entire ideologies and jurisdictions, making you choose a different parking place, or making you go through an entire spiritual ritual before actually parking the car, for increased success, while hoping for a larger insurance claim if you fail, since you know how to ask for more.

Animals have different inner replicas of this world, because by lacking third level intelligent conceptual language, animals cannot understand, share, and teach third level intelligent conceptual knowledge. In this manner, animals cannot understand intelligently individual, elemental conceptual environmental conditions, but only entire environmental chunks at a time, in a second level intuitive manner, exactly how these affect them. This is why the second level intuitive thinking is formed of knowledge and feelings linked together, because this is how the environment makes you feel through all its good or bad conditions, and this is what you must always remember everything in order to be able to avoid the dreadful feelings, while seeking the good feelings instead. In this manner, you seek the adequate knowledge and the adequate achievement, while avoiding the dreadful knowledge and the unsuccessful occurrence, keeping everything within the meanings of life, while never going against Life and the real world, maintaining the second level harmony with everything and everybody else.

Humans also have a second level intuitive thinking, behavior, meaning, achievement, and interconnectivity, made possible by the second brain, which is the reptilian brain or the midbrain, placed right below the cortex. You reason, behave, interconnect socially, and live your life at the second intuitive level throughout all circumstances involving feelings, as all your intimate circumstances, and significantly more.

Even throughout your third level intelligent cognition, you still use second level intuitive thinking taking place in your midbrain in parallel with your third level intelligent cognition from the cortex, for a comprehensive rational cognition, allowing humans to fulfill Life both at the second intuitive level and at the third intelligent level, which is an achievement for any living being or intelligence. However, humans use the entire human cognition, interaction, and meaning at the zero addicted level and at the first consensual tyrannical servitude level, against the meanings and fulfillment of Life, going against Life, humanity, and the real world in this manner, to make drugs, tyrants, and entire dark ages possible, throughout an entire dreadful existence, since this is the current human condition, dreadful.

You have the same intuition as all animals do, yet even your second level intuition is more developed than what animals have. You have three replicas of this world, each one made by your three inner selves from your conscious mind, found in three different brains, placed one on top of another on top of another. This is how the organic life had managed to form your mind and brain ever since the invertebrates, with three brains one on top of another. Your first reflexive brain gives you your first level algorithmic reflexes. You may take your hand close to your eyes right now, just to see and feel how your first reflexive inner self from your basal ganglia in your first reflexive brain closes your eyes without your willing decision as a third intelligent inner self from the cortex. Because your first intuitive inner self from your first reflexive brain precedes you on your lifeline of existence, doing everything in the outside world through you as it pleases. These are your raw reflexes, and it is very important to consider them, since your first reflexive inner self is still one of your selves, it is still you.

Furthermore, you have your second reptilian intuitive middle brain, having your entire second intuitive inner replica of the world, placed on top of your first reflexive brain. Within your second intuitive inner replica of the world spanning the second reptilian middle brain, you have all objects, subjects, and circumstances memorized while linked rigidly with good or dreadful feelings, depending on circumstances. This is how you make your second level intuitive mental models as the second intuitive inner self from the left hippocampus, by choosing the best strategies in order to make you feel the best when you implement them in real life.

This is how all lizards, chickens, dogs, and rats think, intuitively, at the second animal level, by making all decisions according to how they feel or according to how they will feel. Many times, not even having to think consciously, because these second level intuitive conceptions act, think, and react on their own, very fast. Along with their first level reflexes coming from the first brain and through the first reflexive inner self, the entire activity and behavior in the outside world is done very fast and relatively successfully.

Even the second level intuitive conscious cognition is not enough for the organic life, probably because environmental conditions come above the second intuitive level, as you always have to tend to them in an intelligent manner at the third environmental level, and even in a superhuman manner at the fourth environmental level and higher.

This is why the organic life develops a new, more detailed brain, the cortex, of a finer cognitive resolution, allowing you to reason directly through third level intelligent conceptual cognitive elements. If you know how to use the human cortex very well throughout your third level intelligent cognition, you can conduct your intelligent reasoning and intelligent mental models continuously at the ultimate cognitive resolution matching directly the natural laws of this world and the tenth level supreme characteristics of Life, Intelligence, and the wider world, while maintaining your meaning and fulfillment within the meanings and fulfillment of Life.

Why do you always have to maintain your meanings and fulfillment within the meanings and fulfillment of Life? Is Life actually the Deity himself? Yes, from religious and spiritual perspectives, while Life is everything alive from living perspective, intelligence is everything alive form intelligent perspectives, the wider world is everything existent from objective perspectives, while Interconnectivity is everything interconnected as One. Life, the Divine, Intelligence, the wider world, and Interconnectivity are the supreme perspectives of the same oneness, only seen from different existential perspectives, because existence itself is relative, made in this manner by relativity itself. This gives you the choice throughout your study to focus on Life, Intelligence, Interconnectivity, the wider world, or the Divine, depending on your topic of study, while also studying the other supreme perspectives implicitly, because they are the same, as one.

Currently, our topic of study is the human cognition, involving mostly living, intelligent, interconnective, objective, and spiritual perspectives, which are all the supreme perspectives, making our study very dense, very elaborate, and very diverse.

All living beings of all types and forms of life from all worlds and realities form Life, but only if their meanings and fulfillment address Life directly, remaining part of the meanings and fulfillment of Life. Otherwise, they form something else, as entire ideologies, jurisdictions, dictatorships, and communities of addicts at the first consensual level and at the zero addicted levels outside Life and the real world, or entirely against Life and the real world. You already know your second level intuitive and third level intelligent human meanings and fulfillment for Life and the real world, because all your needs and feelings address these directly. Additionally, you have your addicted and consensual needs and meanings that do not address Life and the real world anymore, yet you still fulfill them in an entire consensual world. While you still have your choice to fulfill tyrants and addicts within the Consensual Matrix, or to fulfill Life in the real world, and you always choose tyrants and drugs, ruining an entire world. Life and our Creator gave you this entire world, while you trash it with drugs and tyranny, for your own enjoyment, because once our Creator shuts down this world, you can go in all the other worlds to take drugs, because they are everywhere.

Life is alive through all her living beings composing her, because all her living beings giver her life through all their meanings and fulfillment for her. You are similar, because your own cells and cellular components give you life, through their own life and through their own specialized meaning and fulfillment within the human organism. Life is only your harmonious interconnectivity allowing you to interconnect meaningfully and fulfilling with everybody else. Life is also the living union between the living beings composing them, giving them a continuous living meaningful point of reference allowing them to maintain their continuous harmonious interconnectivity by maintaining their meanings and fulfillment within the meaning and fulfillment of Life. Only in this manner, all living beings can maintain their harmony, never ending up one against another, which would be dreadful.

As you study all your cells and cellular components closely, you notice how they never work one against another, but only in a meaningful fulfilling harmony with each other, as they count in zillions. They are flawless in their entire specialized fulfillment within the organism, by making sure continuously that their meaning and fulfillment remain within the meaning and fulfillment of life. Otherwise, they become negative conditions of the entire environment, and the other cells and cellular components must deal with them, as all living beings deal continuously with all their negative environmental conditions.

It is different in society, because the current society is only consensual, made only for corporations and jurisdictions, not for living human beings. As corporations, all living human beings are made to act one against another in a hierarchic social manner, rendering everybody a negative environmental condition for everybody else, while determining everybody to compete, profit, discriminate, fight, exploit, and exterminate each other, randomly and in a very specific hierarchic social manner, through the entire social hierarchy and social division into social classes. While currently, social hierarchy and social division into social layers and social classes are considered the pinnacle of the human civilization. The tyrants, megalomaniacs, and dictators also consider themselves the pinnacle of the human achievement, human civilization, and human life, yet always remaining dreadful human conditions of the human world, with all humans determined continuously to serve them, while in this manner remaining themselves dreadful human conditions of the human world itself. When you have human beings as negative conditions of the human world and of humanity altogether, there is nothing that you can ever do to save humans from themselves. This world is already dead, regardless if it still takes some time for our Creator to close it down. Yet you must have a cortex allowing third level intelligent cognition in order to realize this entire dreadful human cognition.

You have three brains, three replicas of this world, and three inner selves, which may be avated as genuine avatars by your conscious intelligence to perform its normal cognitive tasks throughout its normal conscious cognition, depending on circumstances. However, from among all these inner selves, you associate more to your third intelligent inner self from the cortex, since only your third intelligent inner self is capable to offer you the necessary intelligent awareness of who you are. It was more logical to associate yourself with an inner self preceding this, since in this manner, you have intelligent conscious access to your entire brain, reflexive and intuitive brains included, yet you cannot even conceive anything intelligently within your first reflexive brain and your second intuitive reptilian brain, by lacking the necessary third level intelligent cognitive matrix making intelligence possible.

We have seen three different inner replicas of this world, one of the third, intelligent human level, one of the second, animal intuitive level, and one of the first reflexive level. While right now, you may state that the third intelligent replica of the world from the cortex is the best, only that all your replicas of this world are complementary throughout cognition. The first two inner replicas of this world are innate, which means that they contain reflexes and intuition coming from previous generations and previous species.

Everything was perfect, the entire human cognition, allowing humans to live life at the third, intelligent human level, in an intelligent human society, part of an entire intelligent human environment, allowing everyone to cope with all third level dreadful conditions that Life and the wider world could ever manifest, while allowing humans and humanity to develop past the third intelligent human level just as well. Only that this fell in the Consensual Matrix, as this is consensual, ideological, juridical, hierarchical, and therefore totalitarian, at the first consensual level, keeping everybody underdeveloped at the first consensual servitude level or at the zero addicted level, and now this is one of the most dreadful conditions in life and in this world. While it seems that it is only a first level consensual condition, since this is what the current consensual society seeks to imply, but it is a dreadful condition of the seventh level, the worst that can ever strike our world, since the Consensual Matrix is kept instated in most of the wider world through seventh level higher abilities, while you are no match at your third intelligent human level or below.

At the first, consensual, ideological, juridical level, you have first level consensual, algorithmic, servitude, ideological, hierarchic, and juridical inner replicas of the world, where you store memories and knowledge in general in very large chunks, as stereotypes, laws, beliefs, and personal convictions. Yet you do so directly in your third intelligent replica of the world from the cortex, compromising it and decaying it to the first ideological level. In this manner, only one percent of the human cognition is accurate, with the remaining ninety-nine percent erroneous, compromised, ideological, inaccurate, irrelevant, diverted, dilapidated, intoxicated, indoctrinated, enslaved, enforced, overruled, tyrannical, and corrupted, while this is a major dreadful human condition.

You have to memorize and think through these consensual cognitive elements throughout life, because everybody does so, because you are better accepted socially when you do the same, because your ideological beliefs demand you to do so, and because you are not capable to elaborate anything that you encounter in conceptual elements because you do not understand these, and therefore you cannot achieve a third level intelligent replica of the world.

When you study people's replicas of this world, you find them mostly underdeveloped, erroneous, stereotypical, and less elaborated, making them very inaccurate. If science helped and provided accurate knowledge to everybody, then people could have gathered all accurate, pertinent cognitive means to develop and to make this world a better, more developed, and more harmonious place.

How exactly can you tell that your actual meaning in life as a living human being is to live your life in this better, egalitarian, utopic place, while neglecting having fun? How can you know that you have to make this world better for you and for the next generations, mostly by sacrificing yourself in the process, by not taking drugs and by not being a tyrant anymore? As already stated, everything that you do in life you do to fulfill your needs and meanings, which means that you do nothing else but fulfilling your needs and meanings. This is the case throughout normal, living environments, because within consensual environments, you have consensual conditions to obey, as rules, duties, and assignments, and you have to fulfill these before you fulfill your actual natural needs and addictions. Yet within normal, genuine, living environments, as in the family or within your entourage of friends, wherever the Consensual Matrix cannot penetrate, you still fulfill only natural needs and meanings, even at the third intelligent human level.

Many of these natural needs are developmental, determining you to tend to your comprehensive environment, while making it a better place, at the third, intelligent human level, since you are an intelligent human living being. Furthermore, without drugs and servitude involved, and with all your second level animal needs assured, you have to invest your entire life in developing yourself and your entire environment, making it better, since you obtain your entire fulfillment in this manner, and this is how you feel fulfilled continuously. This a normal human developmental need, and you always have it in you.

As you read this book, you live your life at the intelligent human level, since this book makes you reason at the intelligent human level, by shifting you to the conceptual intelligent learning mode of life. You feel third level intelligent human fulfillment, since you are rewarded at the third intelligent human level with third intelligent feelings of love and happiness, for your success in finding new accurate intelligent knowledge. Third level intelligent feelings are better than zero level addictions, and better than second level animal physiological fulfillment, with no hangovers.

How do you know to seek intelligent human fulfillment? You have these needs in you, since all developmental intelligences are always in you, ever since the golden ages of Earth when they developed the human cortex. With the Consensual Matrix out of this world, everybody managed to develop at superhuman fourth and fifth levels, with all higher abilities assured. Currently, these developmental intelligences are still in you throughout the cortex, since they are the cortex itself, pushing you to develop yourself, your loved ones, and the entire human environment. Yet you cannot identify these needs anymore, since you have never considered them, by considering this entire consensual addicted world instead, and you fail them by default. With you punished with boredom and restlessness continuously, since this is how developmental intelligences punish you, but you consider these as your needs for zero level addictions and entertainment, or as social acceptance needs, and you act accordingly, decaying altogether. Because once you take drugs and once you serve tyrants, there is no way back to the third intelligent harmonious human level.

If you ever manage to fulfill your intelligent human needs as you do now while reading this book, if you had made it so far in the book, and if you use all pertinent knowledge to develop yourself and your environment to the third intelligent human level, then the current first level consensual society has the perfect means and assignments meant to erase the third intelligent human environment as you intend to instate, returning this world to its first level consensus and zero level addiction. This is the current human condition, consensual and addicted, destroying this world, with everyone in it. While you cannot even cope with the current consensual and addicted human condition, because if you ever try to do so, you have the entire world against you, and they take you out. You cannot interfere with their tyrants and addictions, because these are all they know of life. You can always develop yourself, since you still have your means, but you cannot force others to develop. Just keep developing yourself, while making sure that you remain a favorable human condition in the world, and if the rest of the world does not develop alongside you, then too bad for the world.

Your development to your third intelligent human level and higher is comprehensive, including your cognitive, familial, social, classconscious, spiritual, and artistic. Your cognitive development is easier to conduct, yet you can always have a harmonious intelligent social interaction just as well. It is similar in your mind, because all your intelligences are always harmonious, or they should always be. Your inner replica of the world is a genuine reality in itself, populated by all your intelligences, who are genuine living beings, since they have a physical body and a genuine intelligence, both representing life. Similar to all living beings, you cannot force your intelligences in any manner within your replica of the world and throughout your entire cognitive system, since they are alive, intelligent, and highly pertinent in their own specialization. You may only cooperate with them throughout life, while understanding their needs and specialization, finding common grounds, and keeping your inner harmony.

You can also make sure that all your intelligences have the chance to develop throughout life, if not, you end up with ignorant, addicted, corrupted, indoctrinated intelligences throughout your cognitive system, and life is not fulfilling anymore. If your current cognition is only one percent accurate, it means that your intelligences are ninety-nine percent corrupted. However, throughout a continuous intelligent harmonious development, your intelligences can develop to the third intelligent level or higher, just as you as a conscious intelligence can always reach the intelligent human level. With development come high abilities and high responsibility, and your intelligences will be more careful with the needs and feelings that they send you, as they will also be capable to cooperate among themselves, and therefore they will be able to fulfill their needs independently from you, giving you more time to tend to your other needs, or more time to tend to yourself and to your environment, to develop and to assure your comprehensive fulfillment at the intelligent human level.

How do societies influence the human reasoning? How do societies determine the transition from animal thinking to human reasoning? Do societies determine the human reasoning directly, or it is the other way around, the human reasoning allows humans to form and live within societies? How do social conditions differ from natural conditions? How does coping with social conditions differ from coping with natural conditions? Let us see.

3 SYSTEMATIC SOCIAL HUMAN CONDITIONS

As a harmonious intelligent human being, you always want to be good, while you are always good if your meanings and fulfillment are part of the meanings and fulfillment of life. It is only through your carelessness, misfortune, ignorance, and inability that you fail at times, ending up harming those around and the entire world. Yet you try to be good and you try to do good deeds in this world, as everybody else. As you study your lifetime achievements, you may tell that you have done mostly good deeds in the world, with those around treasuring it.

Why are people good or bad in this world? Everything relates with how they fulfill their needs. Some people are more offensive while fulfilling their needs, and consequently, now they have more wealth gathered around themselves. In contrast, others gather less material values, but they focus on other matters throughout life, as watching the media, travelling, studying, or taking drugs. What is better to do? Everything depends on the meaning of life. If your meaning in life is to feel good, then you will do so, only to achieve it. If it is to be good in this world, to help others, then you do so, and it is more fulfilling. Yet it seems that no one knows what the meaning in life and in this world are. Your meaning in this world comes in eleven different levels and in just as many classes. This is the case if you are free in this world, because if you live your life in servitude, you have significantly more to do throughout life.

In order to keep your meanings within the meanings of life, you must know first what meanings are. Currently, all tyrants and all ideologies redefine the human meaning, the human virtue, and the human honor to mean and to be exactly what they need them to mean and be in order to serve them. This is only first level consensual ideological knowledge, while at the third intelligent conceptual level, the human meanings are everything that humans do for others, in order to help them fulfill their needs. You will always fulfill needs and meanings throughout life, because you always receive needs and meanings from all your intelligences to fulfill in the outside world.

Your second level physiological needs are easier to identify, since these are your needs to eat, recover, interact socially, reproduce, and save yourself. Your intelligent human needs are mostly developmental and harmonious, making this world a human place.

Additionally to your needs, your intelligences also send you your meanings, yet your meanings are different than your needs, even if they feel similarly, and even if you fulfill them similarly. Your needs address yourself and your family, by fulfilling you closely, while your meanings address those around or even the entire world. Through your meanings, you help others fulfill their needs, while through their meanings, they help you and others to fulfill your needs, making possible the entire harmonious intelligent human interconnectivity, with only favorable conditions coming from your entire interconnected harmonious social environment.

Your meanings address others as they fulfill their needs, making you a favorable condition in this world, integral part of their own niche, which is among your highest achievements. You, through your own meanings, becoming an actual living niche in life and in this world, necessary for others to fulfill their own needs. This is possible only when your meanings and fulfillment are part of the meanings and fulfillment of Life, while in this manner, everybody developed at the third intelligent human level can find and can fulfill any specialized third level intelligent human meaning in life and in the world that they choose, that they are more talented, or that the rest of the world finds more necessary in life and in the world, to help them fulfill their own needs.

From among what you like to do best, what you know to do best, what you are talented more to do best, and what the rest of the world finds more important and more necessary for you to do, you always choose your meanings and fulfillment from among everything that the world needs the most from you.

Everything that you do in life is meant to fulfill needs and meanings. You can fulfill these at the zero addicted level if you choose, by taking drugs as everybody else, or at the first consensual level by serving tyrants and by being a tyrant yourself, to gain the necessary money to fulfill your physiological needs and to buy your drugs, since this is currently the common human life in an undeveloped consensual world. However, at the third intelligent human level, in a third level intelligent human world, throughout entire golden human ages, everything is already set in place to offer you a third level intelligent human life by default, because the entire third level intelligent human environment is always present, never erased, as it is currently the case.

In a third level intelligent human world, all your needs are fulfilled even by default, because countless of people before you had already found their intelligent human meanings in life and in the world, and now all specialized intelligent meanings are already filled up. In this developed intelligent world, it is very important that you find your own intelligent harmonious human specialization, as new, as adequate, and as necessary as possible, otherwise, you end up living an entire life meaningless and therefore unfulfilled. However, the third level intelligent harmonious human world is very diverse and very fulfilling, always allowing you to augment it with your own intelligent harmonious meaning and fulfillment, because it is very vast. This is the actual intelligent human life, intelligent human meaning, and intelligent human fulfillment, always as a favorable human condition, and always part of the life, meanings, and fulfillment of Life.

Currently it is different, because currently, you end up in life and in this world exactly as what your own handler from the entire masonry of this world wants from you. If he wants you to harm and to exploit others in order to increase his own wealth and social influence, this is exactly what you do, while always remaining an unfavorable human condition for the rest of the world, making your own life tyrannical and therefore dreadful. What else can you ever do? Not much. If you are in the current consensual masonry, you must do exactly as told, and you might never develop sufficiently enough to become a favorable human condition in life and in the world.

Study this circumstance closely, to notice how, as any favorable human condition in life and in the world, if you ever achieve it, you end up making this world a better place, while always developing this world, yet in this manner, you end up interfering with the entire system of discrimination and exploitation made possible by the entire current consensual masonry of the world, and they take you out, because through you, they receive less profit and less social power from the lower social layers. Only if you are from the Masses, never part of the current consensual masonry of Earth, you can still have the chance to develop to the point where you want to become a good human condition in life, in humanity, and in the world, because in the current Brotherhood, in the current Elite, and in the entire Consensual Matrix, you are never allowed.

What can you do, at least in the Masses, to be a good human condition in life and in the world? Nobody wants this even in the Masses, because people seek drugs and tyranny the most, not favorable human conditions. However, if you are more developed, and if you already avoid drugs, tyranny, exploitation, dogma, servitude, medication, and food additives, you must always keep your own meanings and fulfillment within the meanings and fulfillment of Life, of our Creator, of this world, and even of the higher worlds where the souls live, otherwise you remain unfulfilled, and you will return to drugs, servitude, doctrine, and addictions shortly. Therefore, it is very important that you find a meaning in life from among the meanings of Life.

If you know exactly how to repair specific issues encountered in all smartphones, everybody having these issues will come to you to help them, while you will always help them even free of cost, because your own intelligences reward you substantially every time you help the others fulfill their needs. Smartphones help people interconnect even harmoniously, with your own help as direct part of their own interconnective niche, and therefore part of Life. It is similar if you are capable to understand very important topics, as Life, the wider world, the Divine, human conditions, intelligent cognition, interconnectivity, and niches of life, because through all your knowledge, you help others develop, while in this manner, your meanings are part of the meanings of Life and of this world at the third intelligent human level.

Because if you have these major intelligent conceptions in an accurate form at the center of your cognition, everything that you understand furthermore on top of them will always be in an intelligent accurate manner, because everything else relates to the major third level intelligent conceptions of life, reality, existence, cosmology, meaning, interconnectivity, success, needs, and fulfillment, making your entire cognition more accurate than the common one percent.

Because if you have the big bang theory explaining the human reality, the human world, the human meaning, and the human life, you cannot have more than one percent accuracy in the human mind, because everything that you learn and understand in life and in the world is based on these, making your entire human condition dreadful in this manner, because with only one percent accuracy in your mind, reasoning, and decisions, everybody else takes the opportunity to hijack you and to make you work for them from then on. This is the first consensual servitude ideological level, and it is very common in an undeveloped consensual world.

Specialized intelligent human meaning is capable to interconnect everybody at the third intelligent human level. If you compare life on Earth with a cruise ship, then everyone on that cruise ship might have the same meaning, to feel as good as possible, before the voyage is over and before they have to go back home. Yet not everybody is a guest on that cruise ship. Some have to steer the boat, others to cook, to manage resources, to read charts, to wash dishes, and to carry goods and materials around, wherever the guests want them. In this specific example, your condition on that boat is how hard or how easy it is for you throughout the voyage, as a dishwasher, as a guest, as a captain, or as a bartender.

Everything is more complex even on cruise ships, because your human conditions never relate to the fact that you have to wash dishes all day long, because this would still be an easy life, allowing you to fulfill all your second level physiological needs and even your intelligent human needs. Your human conditions are more dreadful in an entire discriminated undeveloped consensual world, because they always relate to the manager that happens to hate you or that happens to chase you around for personal gratification, challenging you more. Additionally, they never give you decent sleeping quarters on the cruise ship, but only a very small closet, and that is your condition in this world.

Notice the entire social division on the cruise ship, with guests always served, crew always working hard, and management always being very demanding, in order to maintain this entire discriminant, hierarchic consensus. This is the first consensual undeveloped level, and it is the case in the entire world, not only on cruise ships. Yet are you developed enough never wanting to serve tyrants in the current hierarchic society? Are you developed enough never wanting to be served by the socially inferior people below you in the current hierarchic consensual society? Because you must be a tyrant to accept a continuous servitude coming from the poor and from the socially inferior that you keep poor and socially inferior in every consensual manner, only for you to have someone to pour your drinks, wash your dishes, and polish your shoes. While if your clothes are dirty and wrinkled, you scream at your servants to serve you more, because you find it inadmissible to be served at any low standards, but only at high standards. Are you developed enough to identify your entire tyranny in life and in the world, along with the entire dreadful human condition that you are in life and in the world?

What if everybody was on that cruise ship for such a long time, that they forgot why they were there? What if they forgot their meaning in life, along with their meaning on the cruise ship? Because, by having nothing to do all day, you have an entire boatload of people who cannot really understand why they are there. Beliefs start to spread, while starting entire social and political ideologies, because by not remembering their actual meaning on that boat, everybody starts believing that becoming a captain is the greatest meaning in life. Therefore, everybody tries to take over the boat, to become the captain. Yet since the waiters and the chefs have all the food that they want and therefore all the wealth on the boat, everybody believes that by having entire stocks of food, drinks, and therefore wealth, then wealth is the meaning in this world, and therefore this is what they always seek, to be a chef and a waiter, in order to have more. Others find their way to join the tight employment hierarchy from the engine room so they can always be in control, by receiving and giving orders, and this is how they receive a monthly salary, which is always good, because it gives them something to do, yet always away from the meanings and fulfillment of Life. While from a boatload of guests, you are left with only a dozen guests, those who had never managed to find a place to serve in the entire boat hierarchy, while always feeling meaningless and unfulfilled.

Did any of them ever find out their specific meaning on that cruise ship? No. Did they end up ruining their vacation?

No. Did they end up having a more fruitful experience than whatever you find currently on cruise ships? Yes, certainly. Because as a guest, you are at the zero addicted irrelevant level, always taking drugs and always being served, while never fulfilling Life in any manner. Yet as a crew, chef, or waiter, you are at the first consensual servitude level, which is higher than the zero addicted irrelevant level, yet still apart from the meanings and fulfillment of life, because Life starts with the second intuitive physiological animal level.

If you were on your family yacht instead, with all your family and loved ones around, you were at the third intelligent human level continuously, while you certainly knew your meaning in life and on the boat. However, in this different circumstance, you have to put up with the third level unfavorable conditions of the open sea in a smaller boat, yet you still manage, as you keep developing alongside your loved ones, always having third level developmental opportunities in an entire world, as you go around the world. If you know the human meaning in life and in the world at the third intelligent human level, then you find ways to interconnect with everyone throughout the journey, with the entire world, in order to make a genuine human difference in life and in the world, while becoming in this manner a third level favorable intelligent human condition in society, in life, and in the world, which is what you actually have to achieve in a human world.

Compare this third level intelligent human achievement with whatever you can achieve currently by going on a cruise ship. All you do on a cruise ship as a guest is drink and eat, while as a crew, all you do is serve, with the entre cruise ship meaningless in life and in the world.

At least ferries take people from one place to another, while fishing boats feed the world, making cruise ships a burden in the world, unnecessary human conditions, along with all mega yachts owned by the richest of the world. Who would ever want that? With people starving in the world by the millions, and with the rich and very rich smiling happily from their megayachts, but only one week a year, because they have to go to the other parties of the world in the meantime. They are the dreadful human conditions of the world, ruining this entire world. Your own dreadful human conditions, not theirs, since they never care, yet since you serve them closely, they always reach you, and you always serve them.

Yet you do not have to go around the world on your private yacht alongside your entire family to make the world a better place by becoming a third level favorable intelligent human condition in life and in the world, but you can do so right now, wherever you live, since it counts similarly. Just use your life to better the world, while always keeping your meaning and fulfillment in the meanings of Life, while avoiding addictions, tyranny, and servitude. It is this simple. If you do so continuously, then you manage to live life at the third intelligent human level, as a third level intelligent human condition in life and in the world, which is good.

Yet you are never allowed to apply the meanings of Life in this undeveloped consensual world, because you end up developing this world, while interfering in this manner with the entire system of exploitation of this world. Currently, you must have a license to do anything in this world, including teaching, healing, and feeding this world, while they never give you a license if you teach intelligent accurate knowledge throughout schools, if you actually cure the people throughout hospitals, or if you feed the people with normal nutritious healthy food free of poisonous additives.

The entire human activity is controlled minutely consensually in an entire social hierarchy spanning the world, and you must do everything exactly as told while you fulfill your needs and meanings. You are not allowed to fulfill your needs free of cost, since it is considered theft, while you are not allowed to help others through the fulfillment of your meanings free of cost, because it is considered abuse and harassment, but you must always do everything according to a very specific consensus which is integral part of the entire system of exploitation of Earth. Even if you fulfill your meanings at a cost, you must have a license, in order to operate in this world as a corporation, not as a living human being. Yet they do not give you a license if you want to make this world a better place, because you interfere with the entire system of exploitation if you make this world a better place. You cannot change this if you are in the Brotherhood or in the Masses, mostly if you do not have a license.

You cannot be a good condition in an undeveloped consensual addicted world, but only a dreadful condition, as it is the case with the entire current consensual Brotherhood, with its entire masonry in the West making all drugs and tyrants possible in the West, and with all radical political and religious ideologies in the East making all tyrants and dictators possible in the East. Since most of the world is in the Brotherhood, they do everything dreadful to themselves. Consequently, our Creator ends this world and the rest of his creations above for this reason, since everyone in this world and in his worlds above choose to remain dreadful conditions, compromising and destroying everything, all his creations. Never again.

In an undeveloped consensual addicted world, you are constrained in every manner to remain a dreadful human condition in life and in the world. Everything remains contorted in an undeveloped world, determining you to live your life on lower developmental levels. While you remain underdeveloped, addicted, dogmatic, enslaved, or tyrannical, you are always a dreadful human condition in life and in the world, of all levels.

You do not need entire textbooks and ideologies to develop, because you have within all your developmental intelligences seeking to develop you continuously, through all developmental needs and meanings that they send you. This is why you read these books, by fulfilling your developmental needs coming from your intelligences, and they reward you with good feelings. Additionally, your intelligences love learning more about themselves, rewarding you even more. You always receive needs and meanings, including developmental needs and meanings, and you must always fulfill them, otherwise you are punished with dreadful feelings, and it is bad. You are always punished intrinsically when you are a dreadful condition within your cognitive system, with dreadful feelings. You cannot even remain idle in order to avoid fulfilling your needs and meanings, because your intelligences always punish you.

When you are more developed, you become more capable to fulfill your intelligences, yet you must always avoid the drugs, tyranny, and servitude of this entire consensual world. Your intelligences always develop you in the exact manner that they already know that is best for you, since you have been highly developed before throughout previous ages, species, forms of life, and even throughout previous worlds and realities. Your developmental intelligences remember everything, since they were the ones developing, in this specific manner that they demand from you currently. They are the ones punishing you with this continuous boredom and loneliness, regardless of how rich and successful you are in society, and regardless of how many people surround you in society. Because this is not a human society, but a consensual one, meant for corporations, while this is not what your intelligences want from you.

It might be, with you always happy throughout the tight hierarchies of society. Because as you study this world and as you study the specific history of many parts of this world, you notice how not the entire world experienced harmony, development, and golden ages, but many people of this world had to go through dynasties and totalitarianism continuously, one dark age after another. Since this is why you have dictatorships in the open throughout many parts of Asia, because people are used to it there and can tolerate it casually, as it had always been dreadful, while always dreaming to become rich and powerful themselves, tyrants and dictators themselves.

The problem is not what your developmental intelligences want, since they have been in this world for billions of years while demanding the same from all living beings long before you were born, but the problem is that society comes with laws, rules, and regulations that are only decades old, while Life, the humankind, along with all human intelligences are ageless, requiring that you behave in other ways, at your intelligent harmonious human level, always as a good, adequate, helpful human condition. This contradiction from your natural and consensual needs always harms you, becoming one of your most dreadful human conditions.

Why is society with all its laws, rules, and regulations going against Life? Society goes against Life through you, because society goes against you and against your genetic line very aggressively. When you study all laws, rules, and regulations that those controlling society have created and implemented in society to stop you from reproducing and to stop you from teaching others to reproduce successfully, you notice how everything is meant to kill your genetic line while also killing theirs, only to leave in this world the tyrants and dictators from the East and from the West, with all their genetic lines intact and prosperous. If you persist to reproduce as your own intelligences demand, you are harmed socially persistently, and it might lead to divorce and to jail time, both meant to render your genetic line extinct, because you cannot reproduce on your own while you are divorced, while you cannot reproduce in prison men with men and women with women.

As a reference, you should aim to have four children or more, exactly with the people that you love the most. Because if you have less children, with only one spouse, your genetic mass and genetic diversity are too low to maintain your genetic line, and you are out of the way, you go extinct. Yet since it happens with everybody, you find it normal.

Do you learn these at school? No, never, since this is the dreadful human condition, and it always kills you. You still learn that you get gonorrhea every time you have sex, along with syphilis, and this is all. Then what exactly do they teach you in school? Not much, only gonorrhea, since education itself is a dreadful condition in the current consensual society, while affecting the Masses and the Brotherhood both, making this world a dreadful place. If you assume that the other branches of society are better, this is never the case. What better social branches? Finance? Politics? Economy? Science? Business? Government? Media? Lodges? Medicine? Academia? Space exploration? Everything is fake and diverted until it remains a dreadful human condition.

With the Brotherhood itself making everything dreadful, as it spans the world. Yet this is their world, because most of the world in the Brotherhood, so nobody should ever complain. They should always refer to all these dreadful consensual human conditions as the good human conditions, since everyone loves them. Just do not expect to have more of these worlds from now on, since you have already trashed everything in this entire cluster of created realities, and our Creator is ready to move to something else. Do not bother our Creator with your prayers anymore, because as long as you are integral part of the dreadful consensual human conditions against humanity, against life, against this world, and therefore against our Creator, with you always praying to our Creator to make you rich and healthy in order to harm more, then our is ready to end all these world, in order to move to something else.

The laws of all societies are your most demanding social human conditions. You are always made to believe that laws are absolute and must be respected, or this is what education and justice claim. Yet when you study laws, you find them valid for decades, and then they are changed. What was illegal becomes legal, but no one questions the necessity of the system of laws itself. If you try to speak against them, they charge you through more irrelevant laws, while all unfavorable social human conditions coming through laws and beliefs go against your inner intelligences, since they have other needs for you to fulfill, which are significantly more meaningful according to your entire human nature.

What other needs? Why exactly are your intelligences against social laws? Not against all social laws, yet your intelligences might be against authorities, mostly when your intelligences avoid serving throughout hierarchies at the first consensual level.

Why do you have people capable and willing to serve throughout hierarchies at all levels, harming others and the entire world, while other people stay away from these harmful circumstances, and never harm anyone and anything? Because as stated, genetic lines and entire nations had been through various environments along the ages, some good and some bad, some developed and some underdeveloped, some fulfilling and some not, and now this is what they are capable to do, these are the needs that intelligences send you, and this is what they want you to do. If they have been serving in slavery throughout packs, herds, tribes, kingdoms, dynasties, and totalitarian regimes, now this is what they want from you, while demanding that you find a spot throughout the top of the hierarchy, and this is what they push you to achieve continuously throughout life. This happens with most of this world, because these people have already exterminated the others throughout their quest for social supremacy, while taking all the developed out. Mao, Stalin, Hitler, Mussolini, Lenin, Khan, Kim, and Putin eradicated and still eradicate hundreds of millions of developed people, with all their developed intelligences gone, no more. You have only the docile and the tyrants left, since this is the best combination for both, while this is their world, always undeveloped, and always in dark ages. No wonder our Creator ends this world and the higher worlds where the souls live, because nobody wants to have drugs, tyrants, and dark ages in their creation.

As a reference, if your genetic origins are in Europe, around the Mediterranean Sea, or in some parts of Africa, South-East Asia, and South America, you have known some golden ages of Earth, yet mostly dark ages. Study the ancient history of your genetic line, because if there is nothing there where you grew up, it means that tyrants ruled continuously, throughout continuous dynasties, keeping their slaves and servants underdeveloped.

It is the same currently, because if there is nothing actually valuable, artistic, and historic where you live, that is still tyranny and dictatorship, covert or in the open. These tyrants and dictators are your most dreadful human conditions for you, for those around, and for all your genetic lines. Unless you are a tyrant yourself, just waiting to become more powerful to replace them, since you are happy in this manner in any totalitarian regime. Slavery is a very good condition for you when you are a tyrant, a slave in command, or a slave master, yet you are a dreadful human condition for all the slaves that you control and that serve you, just for you to have someone to cook your food, wash your clothes, and dance in front of you.

Do not wait for the tyrants and dictators themselves to admit that they are tyrants and dictators, since they never do. Instead, they offer themselves wonderful names and titles, as his excellency, marshal, his highness, of the people, and for the people, while even believing that they are wonderful, since this is basic megalomania.

Your social conditions are more complex if you have been through all past environments, since genetic lines intermarry, sharing all intelligences, along with everything that these know, remember, and demand, while they make a specific order, hierarchy, or harmony within your cognitive system. According to your various modes of life, you have them eventually interacting directly with you the conscious intelligence within your inner cognitive sphere, and it is significant that you are able to identify them. You never have to fulfill their needs for servitude and oppression if you find them inadequate, or you fulfill them if you want, since it is your life, and therefore it is your choice.

It is worse when specific ideologies and jurisdictions decide your life through your choices, controlling you and all your intelligences in this manner, since this is your current social consensual human condition, and this is how it manifests. Yet if you have a higher spot within your hierarchies, you might even enjoy it, since your inner social intelligences specialized in hierarchies reward you well for all your consensual achievements, as it happens currently with most of this world.

What exactly are they breeding here?

Is it better to have no authorities, no social control, no laws, no documents, no consensual corporations, and no consensual duties whatsoever? Had these genuine, natural, even intelligent human societies and civilizations had ever been instated in the past, for their corresponding conditional intelligences to be in you now, demanding the same from you? Are these free, natural, genuine environments even possible, or they are only utopic? They are possible, yet you and everybody else must be developed at the third intelligent harmonious human level in order to be able to live a normal human life without the entire consensual bureaucracy of Earth, otherwise, without the current authorities, you take the opportunity to become an authority yourself to enslave the entire world, making everything worse. You already have the third level intelligent human society at home, in miniature, since it is your actual family. Many times, during the good times, your family at home is at the third intelligent human level, and this is the only human environment that you ever have.

Everybody wants to live life in a larger, even comprehensive human family, where everybody can be with everybody for as long as they please. When you study people's activity on the Internet, you find this type of intelligent human social needs and fulfillment, as it is possible only within intelligent human societies, which are actually overall genuine families spanning the world. Yet when you study science, education, media, history, and entertainment, you find only very small human families accepted, or only couples, or one individual alone altogether, as it is the case with everybody currently. Even animals are depicted throughout cartoons as living life alone or in couples, having only one cub, and being very happy. While the Upper Brotherhood and the Elite live life in genuine overall human families, developing exponentially and taking over this world, not only through extraordinary wealth, military power, higher knowledge, and social control, but also in very large numbers, because they reproduce exponentially, and now this is their world. While the

Masses and the Lower Brotherhood atrophy, because this is not their world, according to the entire hierarchic social consensus of an entire undeveloped consensual world, but it belongs to their authorities, to those in control. This is why there are authorities in this world, to have this world.

'Anarchy' is an old Greek term coming from the old times, and it means no authorities and no laws. Similarly, within egalitarian societies, there are no authorities and no laws, and everybody is equal, with everybody taking an equal share of everything, or taking any share, as much or as little as needed. You might claim that this can never work, since you are made to believe in this manner through all crimes that you see in the media, but study intelligent harmonious human societies closely, to find them resembling normal human families at home in private.

Why are normal families viable and even at the third intelligent human level, but utopian societies are not, ending up in destruction, as entire major ideologies and regimes as communism? Because again, families remain instated naturally, through everybody's natural fulfillment, as this assures equality and prosperity within families. Within families, everybody tends to the needs and fulfillment of all family members in an equal manner, since nobody is neglected, discriminated, or exploited within families.

Communism is a social ideology at the first consensual level, and therefore it always remains incompatible with the human nature, human development, human interconnectivity, human achievement, and human fulfillment, as these are at the third intelligent harmonious human level. From its own first consensual ideological level, communism is always a dreadful human condition in the human world.

Etiologically, communism should have always offered everything in common, while this is in itself a third level intelligent human characteristic. Yet ideologically, communism promises to offer only social equality, but never life in common, as in a genuine human family spanning the world. While in real life, communism does not offer even social equality, but social hierarchy, social classes, and therefore social division and social exploitation, while making possible a multitude of tyrants and dictators throughout the upper social communist layers, feeding on the rest of the world below, through an entire radical communist political party. While humanity was supposed to be an entire family spanning the world, with all its members, the entire world, equal, developed, meaningful, and fulfilled, at the third intelligent harmonious human level.

This is what communism, capitalism, and all ideologies, politicians, governments, and regimes of the world past and present promise but they never offer, the possibility for everyone in the world to remain a favorable human condition for everyone in the world at the third intelligent harmonious level. This becomes the case only when everyone in the world is allowed to tend to everyone in the world, just as everyone in your family tends to everyone in your family. You do not only divide resources and workforce equally, but you make sure that everybody is capable to fulfill all their needs, because without fulfilling their needs, they can even die. It is your human meaning, part of the meanings of Life, to tend to everybody else while making sure that everybody is capable to fulfill their needs, exactly as you do at home in the family. This is more than social equality, but it is intelligent common harmonious human fulfillment, impossible in a disconnected world into small lonesome families and individual lonesome human beings. You must have an overall intelligent harmonious human family spanning the world in order to have an intelligent human world, with only proper adequate favorable intelligent human conditions in the world. Otherwise, you have only dreadful human conditions in life and in the world, compromising this entire world, with humanity and the human development included.

Coincidentally, we notice how all ideologies, politicians, armies, lodges, and governments promise continuously an equal prosperous world, while having an only purpose, to make all tyrants, dictators, and megalomaniacs possible throughout the upper layers of all societies past, present, and future, remaining coincidentally dreadful conditions in the world, regardless of everything that all authorities promise, because they are the authorities, and they seek only their own prosperity, in the detriment of all those below serving them. Coincidentally, this is always the case in all nations, past and present, throughout all worlds of this entire cluster of created realities, higher and lower. Why is our Creator keeping these worlds?

No one ever wonders why all societies are divided in social classes and social layers, since social division in itself remains a dreadful human condition in life and in the world. Because division enhances discrimination, further enhancing exploitation and eradication. No one wonders why social hierarchy and social classes are considered the pinnacle of the human civilization, and no one cares, because everybody serves and is served throughout the social hierarchy, allowing everybody to be a tyrant and to take drugs, unless you are from the bottom social layer where there is no one below to serve you, yet nobody cares about you down there from any social layer above, because no one wants to be in your place. It is dreadful to be you in a consensual hierarchic world on the bottom social layers, until you are exterminated, and those from above the bottom social layers to carry the entire load, and nobody from above ever listens to them either, in a rather coincidental manner. How far exactly can ignorance go in an undeveloped consensual world? As far as it takes to make all drugs and tyrants possible, because this is why all souls come here in this undeveloped world, for drugs, tyranny, and cheap gratification.

As you study history, you notice how your genetic ancestors formed very large armies throughout time, and used them to take over this world in an organized violent manner, forming large empires in the process, and now this is what you have in you, since these are your developmental intelligences. Yet when you study everybody, you find them relatively peaceful, and more developed. It is only when those old, violent traditions and ideologies are still present, that they can harm the world.

As it is the case currently with the entire nonvisible kingdom controlling the West tyrannically. The nonvisible kingdom originated in the Caucasian region in Asia, in Georgia, and migrated in mass to East Europe, and then to the entire West. When you study the Caucasian region from Asia, you find nothing there, since you are never developed under tyrants, dictators, and entire dynasties of these. These leave nothing behind, because they never develop their nations, in order to subdue it and to exploit it systematically. With the nonvisible kingdom on top of the West, you have the same old dynasty still around ever since they were in Georgia from the Caucasian region in the East. It is the same in the entire East, since there were dynasties everywhere in the past and distant past, as there are tyrants and dictators almost everywhere currently, the same ones, of the same tyrannical genetic line both in the West and in the East, the worse human conditions that you can ever have.

Since everybody serves under tyrants and under entire dynasties of these, they make possible yet another dreadful human condition, the comprehensive human stupidity spanning the world, and it never ends, one dark age after another. Currently, everybody refers to the human stupidity as human ignorance, yet it is the same dreadful human condition regardless of how you refer to it. When only one percent of the human cognition is accurate and therefore adequate, with the rest indoctrinated, intoxicated, diverted, contorted, subdued, tyrannical, addicted, worthless, improper, undeveloped, damaged, sick, incapable, and distorted, should this be called stupidity, or ignorance? This is the human dilemma, yet another dreadful human condition in life and in the world.

Currently, the dictators of the East hold most of the wealth in the world, and they use it as a global social power to take the entire world from under the nonvisible kingdom, because the nonvisible kingdom is worthless, while praising themselves for their entire failure. However, with the entire world in the hands of the dictators of the East, good luck to you, because global dynasties will never end in an entire world, as they had never ended in the East, because these are the developmental intelligences throughout all genetic lines, and this is what they always want form you. Yet is it stupidity or ignorance? Which one exactly is?

Can you ever have families as large as the entire human society, with everybody living together in an intelligent harmonious manner, as you do at home in the family? Yes. Study life in all forms of life and classes of life, to find it harmonious and intelligent, with no laws and no rulers, and therefore with no tyrants and no dictators. Why is the current society different? The current society is consensual, made only for corporations and jurisdictions, not for living human beings, and therefore the current consensual society never addresses humanity, life, and the real world, but only corporations and jurisdictions. They replace living human beings with corporations, while replacing the real world with jurisdictions, in order to exploit life and humanity in the real world, while contorting all higher laws stating that all intelligent life should never be exploited in life and in the world. This is the current human contortion, one of the most dreadful human conditions in life and in the world, because when you contort intelligent living beings into consensual corporations that do not even exist in the real world because they are fiat, never there, then you can do with intelligent living human beings anything you want, exploiting them in any manner you want. What else can be more dreadful as a human condition than this, mostly when humans themselves demand to become corporations, every time they apply for their ID cards and for their social security and social insurance numbers? While with everybody knowing well this cheap trick meant for exploitation, is this actually human stupidity or human ignorance? Which one is it?

You do not have to divorce society in order to avoid the current harmful conditions coming from society, because your share of everything, the entire human niche is still there in society, and without it, you cannot subsist. Because society took over your entire existential human niche, and through it, it took over all your means and opportunities that you have to fulfill your needs in order to subsist and to develop in life and in the world.

You cannot stay and you cannot go, while you cannot change society, so what can you do? Nothing, because everything is designed for you to remain incapable to avoid the comprehensive human exploitation spanning the world, in a dreadful human condition spanning the world. Everybody is in the current consensual masonry, and therefore everybody knows it well. Once you are on the bottom social layer, you remain on the bottom social layers, while no one cares for you from the above social layers of society, because everybody exploits you systematically from all above social layers.

This is why social hierarchy and social classes are considered the pinnacle of the human civilization, because this hierarchic social division makes possible the entire social exploitation and social eradication considered the pinnacle of the human development and human civilization, while they are the most dreadful human condition, always unavoidable in an entire undeveloped consensual human world. This seems more as human ignorance than human stupidity.

Yes, it is certainly human ignorance, not human stupidity, because nobody knows that they are actually a dreadful human condition in an entire human world when they exploit an entire world below from their higher social layer, while ruining an entire world, because with those from the social layers above exploiting them similarly, the entire humanity exploits and eradicates the entire humanity systematically, by legacy, while making all drugs and all tyrants possible. This is certainly human innocence itself, never human stupidity.

How can it ever be human stupidity, when humanity never even realizes what it harms, exploits, and eradicates itself? Yet there is one slight difference between innocence, ignorance, and stupidity. Innocence and ignorance still have care, while throughout the current consensual masonry, care itself is burned with all ceremonies, in order for humanity not to care about humanity, while transforming innocence and ignorance themselves into stupidity, the actual human stupidity, one of the worst human condition in the current consensual human society. Yet from all these dreadful human conditions, which one exactly defines the current humanity the most? Should it be stupidity, exploitation, extermination, servitude, tyranny, contortion, bureaucracy, addictions, politics, underdevelopment, indoctrination, inadequate consensus, discrimination, austerity, pollution, war, waste, or megalomania? Which one should it ever be?

All environmental conditions are classified into distinct eleven levels, while the human competency is also classified in the same eleven distinct levels, always matching them. All natural conditions should always remain at the first level within societies, which means that societies should always assure that the natural environment never bothers humans, not even when it reaches accidentally the third unfavorable level. Through continuous development, genuinely developed humans should always gather third level and fourth level knowledge necessary in developing third level and fourth level technologies, as free of cost energy generators, and agricultural and transportation drones tending to all human needs. This gives humans the necessary time to remain developed at the third intelligent harmonious human level, while tending to all third level intelligent harmonious human needs and meanings, while making this entire world intelligent, harmonious, and prosperous.

Yet none of these is possible in the current hierarchic consensual society, because if it was, you could not be controlled and exploited anymore, and all tyrants and dictators had to live life harmoniously and intelligently alongside everybody else, while fulfilling their needs as everybody else. Yet since this is never what the tyrants want, it will never happen. Additionally, there are no drugs at the third intelligent harmonious level, while everybody wants drugs, the entire undeveloped humanity. This is why the souls come here in this undeveloped world, for drugs and tyranny.

The consensual society develops the human competency, yet only to the first consensual level necessary to serve consensually, not to the third intelligent human level necessary to overcome major third level dreadful environmental conditions, as major pandemics, dreadful climatic changes, and nuclear winters. The consensual society is more difficult and more tedious to cope with than the natural environment of Earth, yet people have to join the consensual society, since they are forced to do so, through lack of resources, because the consensual society took over all human niches, and humans cannot survive and subsist without them. However, humans can never develop in the consensual society past its own first consensual level, and will never reach the third intelligent harmonious level as they always should, in order to be able to fulfill Life at their third intelligent level through all their third level intelligent specialized meanings that are always part of the meanings of Life.

How exactly could humans ever overcome dreadful third level environmental conditions as pandemics, nuclear winters, climatic changes, and falling asteroids? Do asteroids actually fall on Earth? All major pandemics are actually instated deliberately in an undeveloped exploitive exterminating consensual world, since they are grown in a lab, while all nuclear winters can be easily avoided at the third intelligent harmonious world, because nuclear technology is never used in a third level intelligent human world. All climatic changes are triggered by the Sun, not by humans, as it is stated in an undeveloped consensual exploitive human world.

Major climatic changes are dreadful third level human conditions, caused throughout the entire lifecycle of the Sun, yet the Sun affects the entire Solar System similarly, not only Earth. All stars undergo similar lifecycles varying the intensity and the spectrum of their radiation, affecting their entire stellar systems. Here in the Solar System, Mars became void of organic life through dreadful climatic changes caused by the Sun, with all Martials incapable to cope with this major Martian third level dreadful condition, by losing or by never reaching their third intelligent harmonious level, through various consensual constraints also present currently here on Earth.

All dreadful climatic changes are third level dreadful astronomic environments, coming from the tilt in the axis of Earth, form Earth's precession, from the distance between Sun and Earth, which always changes, and from the variation in the intensity and spectrum of Sun radiation reaching Earth, which is integral part of the lifecycle of the Sun.

Even major climatic changes are easily avoidable at the third intelligent human level, by controlling continuously the albedo of Earth. Yet you must do so at a global level, by modifying continuously the color of Earth according to all climatic changes coming from the motion of Earth and mostly from the Sun. The color white has the highest albedo, capable to reflect infrared electromagnetic radiation coming from the Sun the most, while all the other colors absorb or reflect infrared radiation more or less, depending on their own albedo. Lite colors have a higher albedo, and dark colors have less albedo. You can change the color of Earth easily by painting all roofs and pavements white or black in the entire world depending if you want a cooler or hotter climate. If you want a cooler climate, you paint more roofs and pavements in white. If you want a hooter climate, you paint more roofs and pavements black, yet you must do so at a global level, because if people paint these randomly of if they paint them one against another, you never achieve to control the albedo of Earth. It is easier to use solar panels that are darker or lighter in color on top of all roofs and all pavements in order to change the albedo of Earth.

Similarly, you plant crops that are lighter or darker in color if you want a cooler or warmer climate. Yet you must coordinate the entire change of the albedo of Earth at a global scale, which is always possible at the third intelligent harmonious human level, because at the third intelligent human level, the intelligent human competency spans the world. You must also transform all deserts into pastures and orchards, because pastures, forests, and orchards have a higher albedo than deserts, while there are many intelligent procedures to change all deserts into pastures, gardens, and orchards.

Currently, only humans can reach the third intelligent level, and therefore only humans are capable to overcome all third level dreadful environmental conditions on behalf of all life on Earth, not only on behalf of Humanity. This is the actual third level intelligent harmonious human meaning in life and in the world, to tend to this entire world at the third intelligent human level on behalf of all life of Earth, which is always part of the meanings of Life. This is why Life brought here intelligent human beings, in order to tend to this entire world at the third intelligent harmonious human level, because this is why all human organisms have a cortex, always capable to offer third level human rationality.

If your entire society is developed at the third intelligent human level, with no social classes and no social layers, but with everybody living life in an overall human family spanning the world at the third intelligent human level, then everybody is a good condition to everybody else, as it is the case with you at home in the family. Yet with an entire society underdeveloped, and with everybody a dreadful condition in the world, all humans fail their human meaning in Life and in the world, while failing all life, and this entire world. The Martians had already lost their world in a similar undeveloped consensual manner, and now it seems that Earth is next, happening similarly, defining entirely the human stupidity, exactly as it happened on Mars.

Is there a difference between the dreadful human conditions coming from humans themselves, and those coming from the natural and astronomic environments of Earth? All human conditions are mostly dreadful when you live in an undeveloped consensual world, yet they become significantly more dreadful when you have both underdeveloped and the developed people sharing the same world. As you study the current society closely, you notice how everybody is developed at various levels, with the current society eradicating persistently all developed people, their families, and their entire genetic lines, to increase austerity through stupidity, and to render this world significantly more exploitable and more profitable. This is a major dreadful human condition, because by eradicating the developed, you eradicate all capable developmental intelligences making humanity possible so far, and without them, you eradicate humanity altogether, because the remaining undeveloped genetic lines are incapable to cope with all major dreadful environmental conditions.

Consequently, nobody is developed at the third intelligent level, but everybody takes drugs and remains irrelevant at the zero addicted, entertained, irrelevant level instead, feeding on the rest of the world. You are always a burden and a dreadful condition in the world at your zero addicted irrelevant level and at your first consensual tyrannical, servitude, ideological level.

While everybody is at the first consensual tyrannical servitude ideological level, including the entire Brotherhood and the entire Consensual Matrix, as these span this world, the worlds above where the souls live, and most of the wider world. While these ruin life and the world, since from your first consensual servitude level, you unleash all possible dreadful conditions in life and in the world.

There are two ways to cope with social conditions, harmoniously and offensively, and therefore, there are two ways to interact with everybody else, through win – lose, and win – win circumstances. Developed people make sure that everybody wins all around as they fulfill their needs, while underdeveloped people will fulfill their needs in every manner, even through offensive win – lose circumstances. One strategy offers harmony and higher level development, and the other offers disharmony and social competition.

Intelligent harmony is specific to all intelligent harmonious human societies, while humans have to maintain it continuously, because everybody must fulfill the same needs, many times similarly. It is better if everybody fulfills all needs together harmoniously, never working one against another. When this brings continuous successful results to everybody, it is called harmonious living together. Harmonious living assures the fulfillment of all needs, at least the fulfillment of all physiological needs, and this assures a decrease in the level of the dreadful natural conditions of the environment. This is why living beings prefer to gather and to live their life among herds, packs, and societies, depending on their level, and this is why Life gathers to form higher and higher forms of life and classes of life, since these are highly successful in coping with all conditions of the environment.

Can the current society cope with all dreadful conditions of the environment? No, and everything that you see in the evening news is a proof. Furthermore, society remains incapable to withstand even third level unfavorable natural conditions, as major earthquakes or major floods, and people die by the thousands sometimes, just for this social lack of success. It is even better and safer to divorce society, only to subsist, if you can ever reach the human niches outside the current society. While those controlling society live in opulence and are capable to withstand dreadful conditions of all levels, not because they are more capable, but because they use the entire society only on their behalf, not on the behalf of the entire society, because that would develop society to the third intelligent level, and nobody would serve them anymore.

This is the most dreadful human condition, deliberate human harm, yet since everybody wants to be a tyrant and to take drugs in the current undeveloped consensual world, it will always be the case, one dark age after another. All tyrants and all those serving tyrants consist the entire world, as they sabotage and disable the entire world in every manner, only to keep it weak, underdeveloped, and disabled, in order to keep it under control, both as a tyrant and as a slave, in a rather astonishing manner, while making possible all human idiocy in life and in the world.

Idiocy is not exactly innocence, ignorance, or stupidity, because idiocy means lack of successful ideas helping you survive, subsist, develop, and prosper, related with a continuous incapability to withstand dreadful environmental conditions of all levels. The human idiocy is closer to our subject of study than everything else, because only the human idiocy creates all dreadful human conditions coming from humans themselves, while only the human idiocy stops you from overcoming all dreadful conditions coming from the natural and astronomical environments of Earth.

At a closer study, you notice how idiocy itself relates more to having only bad ideas in all circumstances throughout life and throughout the world, throughout the fulfillment of all your needs and meanings, also rendering the human cognition only one percent accurate, and therefore only one percent adequate while fulfilling your needs, becoming in itself a major dreadful human condition. If you ever considered nuclear winters, fall of asteroids, and exploding stars major dreadful human conditions, the human idiocy surpasses these with ease.

You can always overcome idiocy by having only good ideas while fulfilling your needs, never bad ideas. However, when everybody else has only bad ideas alongside everybody else, they compromise the entire intelligent human harmony and the entire human success, rendering humanity altogether incapable to withstand all dreadful human conditions. Look what happened to the Martians. It is easy to have only good ideas throughout your comprehensive fulfillment, by being more careful with your cognition, behavior, and social interconnectivity. Because if you maintain these adequate and harmonious, you are capable to overcome even the human idiocy. However, if you take drugs, behave tyrannically, or serve tyrants instead, you might not have only good ideas throughout your fulfillment, while maintaining the human idiocy instated in life, in society, and in this world, continuously throughout all dark ages. Would the dark ages still be around without a continuous human idiocy? No.

Yet are tyrants more idiotic than their servants, or are their servants more idiotic, by serving them? The entire current undeveloped consensual world is divided only in tyrants and servants, and therefore it is tedious to decide, yet it is certain that some or most people do not always have the best ideas while fulfilling their needs. It is enough to take drugs in order to affect your judgment and therefore your ideas, yet with all souls coming in this world for drugs and tyranny, it questions the cognition, behavior, and achievement throughout the higher worlds where the souls live, making them contribute favorable or unfavorable to the entire human condition here in this world.

How can an entire society synchronize its members towards achieving a common goal, and towards maintaining a continuous intelligent human harmony? This is the case within all gatherings of living beings and not only with human societies, because all members of all gatherings, packs, herds, tribes, and societies must share a common language and a common understanding in order to maintain a continuous harmony among themselves. Lower level animals might have a lower level language, formed through sounds, screams, and bodily expressions, allowing the transfer of lower level information, as feelings and objective knowledge, since these are present in and around all animals, and therefore these are significant to all animals as they fulfill their needs.

In contrast, humans and a few other highly developed species are capable to create and use a more advance form of language, capable to transfer conceptual intelligent information, along with objective information, as the words 'probably,' and 'remembering,' and not only simple, objective words as 'tree,' 'cold,' and 'fear.' This specific difference between the two types of language is outstanding, since conceptual intelligent languages cannot only transfer conceptual intelligent information among the members of a society, but they also form the necessary cognitive matrix for every intelligent living being to use throughout thinking, allowing in this manner to form highly elaborated conceptual intelligent mental models throughout the entire human rationality.

The example with parking the car is still objective in nature, while conceptual intelligent social mental models are highly elaborated and highly complex, resembling entire books, movies, and soap operas going on in your mind only to solve a social problem, and this is the case only because living within societies is by far more demanding than living in the natural environment.

What is the difference between natural and social conditions? Social conditions relate directly to your social life, especially to how you fulfill your needs and meanings throughout your social life. It might seem that social conditions and social needs in general are not too relevant and they are relatively easy to fulfill, but this is not the case. How many times, social conditions have stressed you to your limits, because those around were too stubborn, too selfish, or too aggressive throughout their social competition? People even commit suicide only to escape unfavorable social conditions. In contrast, natural conditions tend to be more direct and less complex, developing you at a slower rate. You will always see a difference of development in people who had an easy life, undergoing lower level conditions, compared to people of a more intense lifestyle, who had to cope with higher level social conditions as these manifest throughout the upper social layers.

Why do people choose lifestyles containing higher level favorable and unfavorable conditions? Everything relates with rewards, because as everywhere in nature, once you are capable to withstand tedious and many times unique conditions, you are capable to occupy a unique social, natural, or existential niche, and in this manner, you become the primal or the alpha of that entire niche element, the primal specialist, with everybody else depending on you to fulfill their needs. This is the unique social circumstance rendering you a tyrant if you are less developed, or rendering you an actual intelligent human niche if you are developed at the third intelligent harmonious level.

How do you cope with social conditions? In the exact manner, through high reasoning, through trial and errors, and most importantly, through trial and errors happening in your mind, throughout elaborated social mental models. This might seem tedious, because throughout social mental models, you only play house, you only model society as it happens throughout books and soap opera, with all your intelligences living life normally within your inner replica of the world. When they are finished simulating your specific social circumstance, they give you the result, the final idea, which is an entire social prediction of future social events and circumstances, and how you should avoid or react to them when they take place. This happens every time and in every social circumstance, since if you ever stop reasoning while you interact socially in any manner, then your behavior might drop below social standards, and you might downgrade in social status and social acceptance.

Throughout the current consensual society, everyone that you interact with is a social condition, and you have to cope with everyone accordingly, because the current consensual society is made for districts, courts, jurisdictions, and corporations, but not for living human beings and for entire living intelligent harmonious human worlds.

You always predict all social conditions through social mental models, or at least you try to predict them in this manner, while everyone tries to do the same with you, in order to predict you. Throughout your conversations, you mental model the entire conversation continuously, in order not to become inadequate or too trivial throughout your conversation. You are very careful with what you say and with the manner in which you choose your words, because the slightest mistake could mean social punishment and social marginalization. This is never the case among your best friends or within your family at home, or this might be the case, yet what you say and how you interact in society makes the difference between your social success and your social failure, because you are always a social condition for everybody else, while it is very important that you remain a favorable social condition, in order for everybody else to remain a favorable social condition to you.

However, through your first level consensual assignments in the current consensual society, you are made to harm those around in any manner and for any profit, while becoming in this manner a dreadful condition for everybody else. The intelligent human society is certainly a favorable social environment continuously, yet the current hierarchic consensual society is always in a disguised social competition against you, in order to motivate all its dreadful social conditions that you always encounter. Additionally, the current consensual society is made only for corporations and jurisdictions and only for profit, always exploiting you and profiting on you, while determining you continuously to exploit and to profit on all those placed on the social layers below, and then to channel the entire profit above to all upper social layers exploiting you.

How do you achieve a successful social interaction? You might not be allowed to have a harmonious social interaction in a consensual exploitive society, because you interfere with the entire system of exploitation, and you are punished accordingly. However, if you are more developed, and if you are not in the current consensual masonry, you can interact socially in the most caring intelligent harmonious manner, if you choose. However, you must maintain a caring intelligent harmony not only in society, but also in the family at home, within your entire cognition, and in all your other environments, because all your spheres of influence are correspondent and they affect each other through you.

Within your cognition, you mental model the entire event in your mind, with every conversational subject that you engage, with every word that you say, and with every tone that you use. You mental model everything first in your mind, to see how your inner characters react to everything that you say. You do so very fast, and in this manner, you have time to gather the most successful ideas while you speak. If your audience reacts negatively in your mind, just change the subject, and remain on safe grounds. The problem with safe grounds is that it becomes boring, since it is already known, and this is why you seek to adopt interesting and even controversial subjects, if you are sure that these are successful.

The success of your intelligent social mental model depends on how well you know your audience, for your intelligent social mental model to remain relevant continuously. Everybody reasons socially in this manner, regardless if they know it or not. If they do not know it, then they just talk instinctually, and they only listen to their inner intelligences to tell them when to continue talking and when to stop. Knowingly or unknowingly, this mental soap opera will go on continuously throughout the multitude of your inner realities and everywhere throughout your cognitive system, regardless if you like it or not, and regardless if you want it or not. Because it will keep you awake at night, for your inner intelligences to debate the most successful or the most dreadful circumstances that you have encountered throughout the day. Yet they do so only for very important circumstances, since otherwise, they let you recover. They even force you to join in and to find successful solutions, while the people upsetting you that day are not there with you because you are at home, and without them, you cannot solve anything anymore. Tell that to your intelligences, as they can make little sense of the outside world. As a reference, how much sense can you make of the higher world? How competent is your entire social behavior and social interaction to provide relevant support for a pertinent higher social interaction in the higher world?

What can you do? You have to find all successful solutions in order to apply them in the outside world the next day at work or among your family or friends. You find this solution through the same mental models, only that you participate consciously alongside your inner intelligences while mental modeling repeatedly until you have your successful ideas. Some people take drugs and prescribed medication to quiet their mind, ending up killing their intelligences and their memories, along with entire inner inner worlds within their cognitive system, as these are highly fragile and very hard to create and maintain accurately throughout social interactions. If you take drugs and medication for years, you end up with mental problems, while you remain unsuccessful in society. Yet everybody does the same, it already seems normal, while continuous lack of good successful ideas means idiocy.

Social reasoning will always help you predict all those around by allowing your inner worlds to continue their social simulations throughout all intelligent social mental models. This is how you will always find out everything that everybody around will do or will end up doing. This is the case if your inner worlds are highly accurate and if your entire cognitive system functions at its best, because if you take drugs, food additives, and medication for every illness, then you can never conduct your reasoning with the high accuracy necessary to predict those around, because everybody is unique, and everybody is highly complex.

This is the case mostly with developed human beings, since these are capable to conduct a highly accurate reasoning throughout all domains and not only within society, always at their advantage. You can easily identify these, since they tend to predict and to avoid all problems. Social intrigues never seem to touch them, they always make sure that everybody wins when they interact with them, and consequently, everybody loves them when they are around, and then everybody misses them when they are away. In contrast, people living their life at the second intuitive physiological animal level, will interact in society in any manner, pleasing or upsetting those around, and therefore ending up being marginalized and having to interact only with people resembling them, when their social behavior is accepted, as low as it might be. This does not mean that some people are better than others, yet despite of what people might claim, everybody discriminates everybody when they are in society, since everybody may choose to be or not in the company of anyone around. When everybody behaves in this manner, then this is how marginalization occurs. You will feel it badly when it happens to you, and this is a major dreadful social condition.

Humans of the second animal intuitive level are not always aware of their entire inner replica of the world, with their entire inner mind soap opera corresponding the entire society from the outside world. They cannot even distinguish between their own inner replica of the world and the outside world, and therefore they end up living their life assuming that everything that they know and understand about the outside world is accurate, while their thinking might be full of beliefs and social stereotypes instead, since all their knowledge about the outside world might be superficial or erroneous. These are the people judging you according to your car, clothes, bank account, wife, job, color of your skin, and speaking accent. They might not even judge you consciously, but their inner intelligences do, through their inner mental models of the outside world, which might be more or less accurate. While with them unaware that they are fed results and social solutions subconsciously directly through their inner intelligences, mostly through social needs, they always do as these inner social intelligences demand, they are rewarded in the process, it is not always adequate in the outside world yet it still works, and the next day, they wake up to everything all over again, subconsciously, while never understanding their own reasoning and implicitly their own social behavior. Science and psychology know nothing in this field, therefore humans can never learn anything about themselves, and therefore they fail to develop.

Developed humans will always be successful in society and throughout life, while less developed humans should always be marginalized, and should always suffer of all dreadful social conditions, which is not exactly the case. Because in a consensual undeveloped hierarchic world, it is never a matter of your own development, talent, interests, and abilities, but it is always a matter of your legacy, wealth, social class, and social layer. The higher is your social layer representing you, the more successful you are in this world, but only up to the level of your social layer. Because all people, developed and underdeveloped, gather into social classes and social layers, as hierarchies, nonvisible kingdom, political parties, religions, social classes, societies, parallel societies, and entire covert societies, as the entire masonry of the West. The higher and the more successful these classes are, the more socially advantaged their members become, despite of their own cognitive developmental level.

If you are a highly developed living human being, you may compete successfully among anyone else in society, and you will always remain among top social layers, throughout your own cognitive development. However, as an individual, developed or not, you can never compete against entire brotherhoods and hierarchies, regardless if you are more developed and more capable. Because through their number and their summative resources and opportunities, they single you out, they marginalize you, they veto you out, and you have no chance. This is how lodges, brotherhoods, cults, and ideologies work, through their number and synchronous dogma and beliefs.

Yet even the strongest brotherhoods have no chance against the nonvisible kingdom. Do some research to identify its members counting in hundreds of millions or probably more, and you will find these sitting on top of everything in the West, owning everything, including you, your family, and your dog. What chance can you have against these people? What chance your local lodge has against these people? It is the same with the tyrants and dictators of the East, since no one can cope with them, East and West.

Because this world is not exactly divided into nations or political and social ideological axis of power as you can see in the news, but this world has a different structure and meaning than what you learn in school. Society manifests unfavorable social conditions that you never expect, because your inner replica of the world lacks the accurate information about this world, being incapable to start your mental simulations and predict average future outcomes. If this world and society start surprising you through their casual events, if you cannot predict anymore any of these, this is the case because you fail to create an accurate replica of the world in your mind, including an accurate replica of society. This world is already globalized and has been in this manner since the end of the world wars. This was the meaning of the world wars in the West, to accumulate all world power for the Rothschilds, who are the royalty of the nonvisible kingdom. There is a genetic extermination ever since, everything that the nonvisible kingdom consider inferior, unwanted, or abominations, which is the rest of the world. While religion is only a mask. Yet the world order had changed again recently, with the dictators of the East on top, after they took the entire world from the nonvisible kingdom, because nobody wants to be exterminated and to be called an abomination. Yet it is hard to tell if it is better to be under the nonvisible kingdom or under the dictators of the East, after all these people eradicate the world genetically by the billions. What should it be better? Hard to decide.

As long as you have major dreadful social conditions as genetic extermination, as long as you and your family happen to be on the unfavorable side of the genetic pool of this world, and as long as your social layer is lower in level than the entire nonvisible kingdom and the dictators of the East, then any condition that you may attempt to tackle currently becomes irrelevant against this major dreadful social condition, because nothing, no problem seems to be more important than global genetic extermination, called genocide. Therefore, if you are still wondering if such and such president was better in fixing the economy, if people should take to the streets and start rioting against the increase of taxes, or if you are still upset because the gas prices increased three cents last month, these irrelevant conditions are fed systematically to you in order to keep you diverted from what it is actually going on. Tyranny and genetic extermination in mass. Who are these people?

What can you do? Stop killing people. Stop the genocide. You are doing everything, not the nonvisible kingdom, but you. The nonvisible kingdom is the beneficiary, while you are the servant, always harming the world. There are no members of the nonvisible kingdom fighting in wars, since the nonvisible kingdom is not even allowed to fight in wars, not even throughout the world wars, but your family does, and it is part of the comprehensive genocide. The nonvisible kingdom does not manufacture war equipment to kill everybody, but you do. If you do not manufacture it directly at your local plant, then you make the smallest components, you only pay for everything with your tax money, you only send your children to war, you manufacture the uniforms, you build the coffins, or you drill for the oil needed throughout conflicts, since it is always you doing everything, neither the dictators of the East, nor the nonvisible kingdom. You vote for the people signing the declarations of war, and you use the money made by the nonvisible kingdom and the dictators of the East, since all money belong to them, along with all nations, all cities, all resources, all people, and including all values that all people have in this world, or this is what they claim.

Are you actually so powerful and so important in this world, even if you are not a dictator form the East? Yes, because you are always a human condition in this world, either favorable or unfavorable.

4 YOU AS A HUMAN CONDITION IN LIFE AND IN THE WORLD

Can the human development be more relevant than any human condition, under any circumstance? Yes or no, because the human condition determines directly the human development. Yet while all human conditions are placed directly by Life in the human existential pathway, the human development alone might not be the ultimate intention that Life has from the human existence. Yet the human development is situated on the same lifeline of causality as the human condition, the human lifestyle, the human experience, and therefore as the human meaning in life and in the world.

We have covered most of the human conditions so far. You can consider the human condition in itself throughout this life as a summation of all human conditions that you may casually encounter and experience throughout a normal human life. You cannot comprehend the human condition directly, because you are not capable to compare directly all human experiences, since you can know only one experience, yours.

Is your condition good or bad in this world? Your meaning in life is not exactly to have good or bad experiences, and probably not even to have a sustained, consistent, successful development, but something else. As seen so far, it seems that the human meaning in life has a collective meaning, not an individual meaning, and it is related to a collective development, more than to your individual development. Whatever it is, it seems that your achievements throughout life do not exactly have a material significance, or a feel good significance, and not even a world supremacy significance, but your achievements seem to manifest in details, in the existential details of this world, and we will see how.

You are the coach of a highly competitive sports team, and your presence and your entire effort in your team makes the difference between winning and losing. Are you a good coach? Certainly, since the results of your team state it directly. Yet are you good or bad with the team throughout training? You are not too good, you are not too kind, and you are not too nice to them, because you are very demanding. You scream at everybody, while forcing them to participate in very hard physical activities, all day. This is called harassment. However, in your gym, you may do as you please, you may be as aggressive and as demanding as you please, and the entire world even loves you for it. You have a talent to harass people, and now you put it to work on your behalf. You seem to be a dreadful condition for the entire team, yet since everybody develops, while always showing results, you are actually a good human condition.

The stronger and the more demanding you are, the more your team develops, and the more capable it becomes while competing with the other teams. All coaches of all teams do the same, and therefore it is only a matter of which coach is the most capable to determine their team to train the hardest, to develop the most, and therefore have the best results.

I study intelligences and hierarchies of intelligences in separate books of this series. As a reference, fourth level good angels will show up to save you when you fall in the river, using their fourth level superhuman abilities to save you. Furthermore, fifth level highly demanding angels will push you repeatedly in the river in order to help you learn how to save yourself, and you will never like it. They never push you directly, but they only create the necessary circumstances for you to fall in the river repeatedly, along with the necessary circumstances for you to be able to save yourself from the river, while learning how to save yourself under all circumstances, developing continuously. All these developmental conditions end up teaching you how to learn to save yourself. It does not matter how many times the fourth level good angels save your life, since they will not be always there to save you, and you will still drown, eventually. Furthermore, with them fourth level angels saving your life every time, you never have the chance to learn how to save yourself. The next time when your life is in danger and they are not around, you die. It takes a fifth level highly demanding angel to teach you how to teach yourself and how to develop yourself.

Fourth level beings represent and are related to good, favorable conditions throughout your life, if these ever show up. While fifth level beings represent highly demanding conditions, yet still benefic. These are not the dreadful environmental conditions seen so far, but only highly demanding developing environmental conditions, which are still good.

Yet you never have to wait for higher beings to influence your life and your development. Your entire experience here on Earth helps you develop, and it is meant entirely to help you develop, not to take drugs and to behave tyrannically. This is important, since it is always in the details, for this continuous experience that your development manifests, condition after condition. When you study it closely, out of your entire experience, many conditions help you develop, and if your meanings are still part of the meanings of Life, they are still good. You might still assumed that Life fights hard to cope with the environment and with all its dreadful conditions, yet Life is the environment itself, and much more, since Life is everything alive everywhere and in all realities, she is the entire wider world with all its environments included, because the entire wider world is alive.

In real life, you want everything to manifest as easily and as peacefully as possible, through all possible good conditions, and through very low dreadful conditions, with central heating and with all cabinets filled with canned food everywhere. Yet when you play your videogames and when you watch your movies, you want these to be as exciting and as aggressive as possible, for an increase in the level of conditions, because it is more fun. It is the same when you ride your dirt bike, since you avoid the roads, because these are flat and easy, but you build an entire dirt bike track in your back yard, full of hard obstacles that you always have to pass in the most tedious manners.

You love your dreadful conditions, but only when you manage to overcome them without being harmed, because they always develop you. This does not mean that dreadful conditions are good because they always develop you, because all human conditions, good or dreadful, are very complex, while you must know them in all details.

The current consensual society has many dreadful conditions continuously targeting you, yet when these eradicate you, your genetic line, and your entire bottom social layer, while you cannot even defend yourself because the entire society above exploits and eradicates you, nothing actually develops you, even if these are the worst dreadful conditions. It is similar throughout your entire exploitation at work and everywhere else, because it develops you only at the first consensual level, teaching you how to serve more and how to be more productive and more profitable, while this never develops you in life and in the real world, but only in a consensual tyrannical servitude manner. The current consensual society is very careful not to develop you at the intuitive and intelligent level, but only at the consensual level, to the point where they fire all capable teachers from North America, while keeping only the consensual ones who serve well and never teach anything meaningful, but only fakery. This is why education in North America is only fakery, several year behind Europe. Consequently, all Europeans are significantly more capable in all domains, with their cars always better and more demanded, similar to the cars from South Korea and Japan, who also have a very good system of education.

You are certainly very demanding as a teacher from Europe, Japan, and South Korea, yet you must know how to teach everything in an intelligent manner, in order to help your students form all their intelligent accurate mental models while understanding everything. Not only the teachers are very demanding and very capable, but the students themselves are very capable to learn everything, while working very hard throughout learning. In contrast, in North America, they use an entertainment curriculum, teaching all students very easy lessons through entertainment, in a rather innocent manner. They even have laws not to give students homework on Friday, in order not to compromise their weekend, while on Monday, all teaching must be very easy, to allow all students to recover from weekend.

There is a specific pattern that we may already notice in our model of the human condition so far, and it is worth studying. Because everything that we have studied here is causal, and therefore we may place it on specific lines of causality. Since Life determines these, we refer to them as lifelines of causality. It is always relevant to form and to study the entire lifeline of causality including all our data and circumstances, in order to be able to find, identify, and understand main causes that determine the entire lifeline of causality, and not only simple effects as significant as they might be, since these are only in the middle of the lifeline of causality, and they do not start it.

If you are incapable to find the main cause determining your illness, you may end up treating a symptom or an effect of this illness, not the main cause, with the entire illness still there, harming you. This is what medicine does currently, and many times, this generates terminal illnesses. When you study medicine closely, you find it owned by the nonvisible kingdom, being used currently as a tool meant for genocide. Let us study lifelines of causality related to the human condition.

Throughout a casual living, your intelligences send you

needs, and this is how everything starts, or this is how everything continues. Because life takes place in cycles, and many times, the cycles never end. You fulfill these needs normally, until conditions change in the outside world. Life uses conditions to determine you to develop in a specific manner, while conditions force you to reason in order to cope with them. You use your reasoning then in order to find a way to fulfill your needs through the new conditions of your natural or social environment. Your reasoning consists of inner mental models that simulate the outside circumstance in order to offer you successful solutions of how to overcome them. You have to repeat your mental model by parts and by stages, until you have your successful solution or successful idea.

Many times, you employ throughout your mental models the same intelligences that send you your needs. Which means that they only need your conscious cooperation throughout the mental model or throughout the actual fulfillment, until they overcome the new condition, or until they are capable to take it from there to fulfill the needs on their own. Because many times, your own primal intelligences are capable to fulfill their needs on their own if they already know how to do everything.

Once you overcome the condition, you memorize the successful solution, and you share it with those around. This is not exactly doing scientific research and publishing all scientific results, but you always mention casually all our experiences while chatting with your friends, sharing all your successful solutions and successful experiences. Yet if your results are not successful, you still share them with those around, only for them not to have the same problems, or only for them to help you solve yours. Your primal intelligences will reward you greatly when you share your experiences and your results with your friends, because this is still part of the human development. While your friends keep on listening, since their own primal intelligences reward them for learning relevant information and for being with you, since you are an enjoyable, reliable company, always eager to help them fulfill their needs.

Next on the lifeline of causality, if you have proven to be

very good at overcoming your specific condition, then others may ask for your help, and you may end up specializing in that specific fulfillment of that specific need, since everybody has to fulfill it but they are not capable to do so on their own, for various reasons. While this might end up being your true specialization in society, your actual meaning, part of the meanings of Life.

You do not actually need money to motivate you to do your meaningful specialization in society, since your own intelligences motivate you through inner good feelings to fulfill your specialized meaning in life and in the world. Yet you are already specialized in society, since you are always eager to help your friends and loved ones, along with all their friends and loved ones with their computers, school problems, car problems, legal problems, shopping problems, health problems, or family problems. You do these as best as you can, but most importantly, when you become very good at any of them, then you have a multitude of people coming to ask for your help, and this is how you know your meaning in life and in the world.

Next on this lifeline of causality is an entire developmental pattern, when you learn as much as you can throughout your specialization. Later on in life, you teach as much as you can to others, so they continue doing what you do after you are gone. You are a good human condition in this manner, an actual living niche helping others fulfill their needs, always part of the meanings of Life, which is very important, because you will always feel fulfilled, in an entire successful human life.

When you study all lifelines of causality affecting everybody, when you study all developmental patterns, all conditions, and all worlds and realities, you notice how Life ends up mental modeling the entire wider world through very specific lifelines of causality and through very specific living beings and intelligences, all performing the same activities while coping with all their conditions and while developing, ending up carving minutely the entire Life or the entire wider world in all possible accurate details, to resemble everything that Life has always intended, in all her supreme conditions and in all her supreme characteristics. How important is to remain a good human condition in all these? Very. How important is to maintain an entire lifeline of causality, with your good human condition included? Very. Yet what exactly are lifelines of causality, and how do they affect life, humanity, and the entire world?

The End

This book series continues with the next book, "Lifelines of Causality." Here is a short synopsis:
We live in an objective world, with almost everything happening everywhere causally, naturally, and fairly. Your entire lifetime activity is causal, since almost everything happening in your life is a continuous succession of causes and effects. This means that, through a highly systematic study, you could be capable to place all events of your life along one line of causality, in order to understand and to predict everything. Since you are a living human being, this is your own intelligent lifeline of causality.
When you study your lifeline of causality closely, you understand why you have chosen and why you have done everything throughout life in this specific manner, in this specific order, and for these specific reasons. Furthermore, through your own lifeline of causality, you understand your own meaning in life, your own meaning in society, and your own meaning in this world, because these also have their own lifelines of causality. In this manner, you are capable to pinpoint the exact interaction between your own lifeline of causality and these comprehensive lifelines of causality, in order to identify, study, and explain all significant events of your life and of this world, how they happen, for what reason, and through what circumstances.
This book studies your life and all significant events influencing your life, how everything happens, and through what circumstances, because everything is always found along

specific lines of causality, since everything is connected. You will understand human beings, society, and this world, along with all higher beings of the wider world.

ABOUT THE AUTHOR

Valentin Leonard Matcas, M.Ed., is a researcher, physicist, mathematician, educator, and an author of nonfiction and fiction books, including the entire "Human" book series. Valentin Leonard Matcas wrote the "Human" book series in the following order: "The Human Needs", "The Human Addictions," "The Hierarchy of Needs," "Stay in Shape, Lead a Healthy Life," "The Human Origins," "The Human Society," "The Human Conspiracy," "The Human Mind," "The Human Reality," "Astral Planes and Your Other Realities," "Life," "The Hierarchy of Intelligences," "The Human Intelligences," "The Human Thoughts," "Mental Models and Successful Ideas," "The Human Attitudes," "The Human Stereotypes," "The Human Ideology," "Modes of Life," "The Human Development," "Patterns of Development," "The Human Lifestyle," "Heal Yourself," "The Human Civilization," "The Human Religion and Spirituality," "The Human Rights," "Higher Laws," "Natural Laws of the Universe," "Existence," "The Human Condition", "Lifelines of Causality," "The Human Behavior," "Flat Earth," "The Human Environment," "The Human Meaning," "The Human Reasoning," "The Human Interconnectivity," "The Consensual Matrix," "The Matrix of Life," and "The Human Knowledge."
Valentin Leonard Matcas writes about terrestrial and alien civilizations, about life in the universe, the way it develops and intertwines across galaxies, about powerful beings as they control and reshape the universe, and about normal living human beings from Earth caught in this beautiful, wider, outstanding interconnectivity. Valentin Leonard Matcas creates a living, warmer universe in his books, teaming with life and vibrancy, on all levels of existence. Valentin Leonard Matcas also wrote "The Storyteller" book series, including "The Storyteller," "Starship Colonial," and "Unlimited," and "The Culling" book series, including "The Culling," "The Dream of the Dead," and "The Last Man on Earth."

When he does not work on his books, Valentin Leonard Matcas enjoys researching, hiking, swimming, kayaking, skiing, snowboarding, biking, reading, listening to music, and playing strategy videogames. You may discover all his books, videos, and articles.